Alternative Views

Who Said Love, Sex, and Marriage Must Be Complicated?

Look at it this way!

Terry A. Strickland, Jr

P31 Publishing

D1510752

Terry Strickland. © 2019

Because of the dynamic nature of the internet, any web addresses or links contained in this book may have changed since publication and may no longer be valid. The views expressed in this work are solely those of the author and do not necessarily reflect the views of the publisher, and the publisher disclaims any responsibility for them.

ISBN: 978-0-578-53277-6

Printed in the United States of America .

Dedication

I dedicate this book to my lovely wife. It was my journey to find her that gave me the passion to grow as a man and the desire to get closer to God and seek His wisdom to understand courting, a woman's value, and His views on marriage. To my unborn daughter who gave me a reason to write, imagining a bond with you gave me direction. To Steve Harvey, it was your book, *Think Like a Man* that gave me powerful motivation. To Taraji P. Henson, you had a powerful effect on me. Thank you all for your different forms of inspiration.

Terry A. Strickland, Jr
Alternative Views
Look at it this way!

Table of Contents

Introduction

Alternative Views was not intended to give anyone a way of life. The mission is to offer the reader the opportunity to view a few chapters in life from a different perspective.

Your perspective is what you believe, and what you believe alters your behavior, and your behavior determines your reality. Therefore, changing your perspective can control your reality.

My views are derived from my personal experiences and decisions that I have made. This is not to be confused or conflicted with the experiences of my readers.

Superman is Coming

Every man must get to a state of vulnerability when he has no choice but to turn to God. It is at this time, he realizes that he is not as strong as he thought, and the best thing he can do is relinquish that control to God. God has empowered man, but man is not God. This is when God lays hands on him and transitions him into the man he was called to be, which then gives him an alternative view on life that makes it easier for him to walk by faith instead of seeing the world through the eyes of man like he used to. Until a man truly has this intimate moment with God, he will always fail to live up to the standards set by a woman seeking a man of God.

Alternative Views started for me when I was facing the woes of life at an early age. I was a 20-year-old college student and a new father in a failing relationship. I struggled to keep a job, and that didn't help my relationship at all. The mother of my child and I were always at odds with each other. We would argue and fight about every little thing, not realizing until it was too late that we were not compatible. That relationship was really taking a mental toll on me as a man. I felt inferior and extremely low. I blamed everyone except myself, not understanding that our relationship status was a result of the sexual nature in which I pursued her. I see now pursuing a woman correctly is imperative to the success of a relationship. Electing not to do so ultimately resulted in me deciding whether I should walk away from this toxic relationship or stay in it just to be with my child. As we continued to fight, the decision to walk away grew more difficult to deny.

I prayed about it and decided the best thing for me to do was to exit the relationship and trust God that I could still be a good father to my son. That decision was by far the hardest decision I have ever had to make. However, shortly after making that decision, it was clear that I was not in the best position in life. I walked away with everything I had to offer, which was nothing. I didn't have any money and wasn't employed, and I did not I have a place to go or family to turn to for help. I did have a car, but when it rains it pours, so of course, it wasn't long before it broke down. My life was a mess. Sleeping in a car was never a part of the plan. I spent days walking the streets from sunup to sundown looking for work with no such luck. I even tried to enlist into the military, but I was not accepted because of a prior D.U.I charge. I needed a commanding officer to sign off on a waiver for me to enlist in the military. The recruiter explained to me that waivers are hard to get, so I returned to my car to sleep. I attempted to keep my spirits high by telling myself, "It cannot get any worse."

Well, I was wrong. It got worse the day I returned to my car, and there was a sticker on it instructing me to move it, or the city would tow it away. I couldn't allow that to happen. I flagged down the fourth tow truck I saw going down the road after the first 3 denied me. I explained my situation, and the driver was nice enough to help me, and with their consent, I towed my car to the house of someone very close to me.

Maybe I should have disclosed to them that I was sleeping in the car. Days after allowing me to park the car there, they decided to have it removed. I do not know why that person made that decision to this day. I was at a loss for words with no idea what to do next. I would go to the gym and spend all day there, I have never felt so alone in my life. I can recall getting so down on myself. I felt low. I spent many nights praying to God with my eyes full of tears seeking understanding. I felt like either God didn't hear me, or He was not listening. I went to the church for help, but my pride wouldn't allow me to explain my situation fully. I wanted nothing more than to just trust God, and just when my faith in God began to sway, He started to work.

I went to church one Sunday with a heavy heart, and at the end of service, the pastor said, "I know a guy that's going through a lot. Step out, I want to bless you." I felt like he was speaking to me, but I wasn't sure. I did not move, and when he said it a second time, and no one else stepped out, I really felt like he was talking to me, and yet I still didn't move. The pastor saw me after church and requested I come to his office. In his office, he said to me, "I know God put it on your heart that I was talking to you. Why didn't you step out?" I said, "I wasn't sure." He responded, "Well, that's how God works. You may never be sure. However, you must step out on faith." The pastor said, "We all miss out on our blessing when we don't," and he wrote me a check for $500.

As I left his office, I kept repeating to myself to step out on faith. No one has ever given me anything in my life. I went to the nearest store and purchased my pastor a thank you card, and I spent a lot of time filling it out, attempting to say thank you in so many ways. I could not wait to give my pastor this card next week. I checked myself into a room that night and took a long hot shower. The good feeling from church today was washing away with the water as reality started to sink back in. I still had no clue what I was going to do. I stood there and filled the shower with tears as I recited "Walk by faith and not by sight." This was difficult, because i wanted to see my progression so bad. I prayed to God to allow me to get a small peek at it and afterwards, I would then close my eyes back and have the confidence to walk by faith, but of course, He does not work that way.

By Wednesday, I was running low on funds but even lower on mental toughness. I grew angry, and bad thoughts ran through my head. The moment I started considering these thoughts it seemed as if the opportunity to act on them presented itself. I was standing outside the hotel that night conversing with another gentleman, and he offered me an opportunity to get some quick money. I told him I would give him my response once I returned from the gym. I knew doing something illegal was stupid and against my better judgment, but I was running low on options. I worked out for an hour before deciding to take the guy up on his offer. However, before leaving the gym, God sent an angel in the form of a beautiful young lady. She was standing at the front of the gym after recently purchasing a membership. I spoke to the young lady, and she was very pleasant. We conversed briefly and instantly connected, and she invited me to Bible study at her church that night. I politely declined thinking to myself I must get back to the hotel to find that guy. I told her I would love to. Unfortunately, I did not have a ride there. The decision was clear to me when she offered me the opportunity to ride with her. I was relieved I was not going back to the hotel to face that decision that had the potential to ruin my life.

I attended Bible study with her that night, and I was introduced to her mother who would turn out to be my amazing mentor who you will read about in a later chapter. The service was more like a social gathering of people fellowshipping together to gospel music. It was more like a party than a church service. The church was completely different then what I was accustomed to. It was a non-denominational, international church. I was used to the traditional Baptist services and not open to change. The entire set up and operation of this church was weird to me, so I left desiring never to return. That Sunday, she picked me up and agreed to visit my church. As we headed there, I began to hear my conscience speak to me telling me we should go back to her church, and I immediately tried to ignore it. The voice in my head got louder, and like the previous Sunday when I was standing in the pew at my church, I found myself again debating with my spirit on what I should do. I thought about what happened last time I decided not to listen to my conscience. As I was debating whether to go to her church or not, a separate voice spoke out to me. The voice attempted to convince me not to return to the other church by reminding me that I had a thank you card I needed to give to my pastor. Convinced for the moment, I could then hear my pastor's voice in my head clearly reminding me to "step out on faith."

I then decided I would give my pastor his card next week. I told her to go back to her church, and we did. The moment I walked into the church everything felt different. Every song that they sang, and every word that the Bishop spoke began to speak into my situation as if he was talking to me directly. I was standing there listening, and before I knew It, I was in tears. I am a very private person so to be crying in public was definitely not my plan, but I could not stop it. When the tears dried up, I can remember feeling relieved and extremely happy. I felt light. It was as if a weight was lifted off my shoulders. It was at that moment I gained the understanding of what it meant to have a breakthrough. I felt so free.

That day, I also learned that I was praying incorrectly for years because I would pray and ask God to change my situation and then wonder why He was not moving. God's focus is not the situation. His focus is you. God does not change situations; He changes people. When life attacks, just pray that God come into your life, and by doing so, you allow God a path to your heart. He then gains access into your situation and changes you in the midst of what you are experiencing.

The key is to relinquish that control and allow God to work on you, and by changing you, you ultimately change your situation by making different decisions. The amazing thing about God is that He can renew your strength and cover you in the midst of your biggest storm. That day, I felt a covering over my life. Nothing about my current situation changed, but I felt different. I felt stronger, and it was as if the situation did not have the same effect on me. The feeling initially was like standing in heavy rain getting soaked. After my breakthrough, it was like standing in the rain with an umbrella, raincoat, and boots, which means you're still standing in the same storm, but the rain does not affect you because you do not feel it.

What a feeling! I ran to the Bishop after church, and after introducing myself, I asked if I could please speak with him. I needed him to help make sense of what I experienced today. He invited me to his office. I stood in the doorway of his office, and before I could say a word, he stated that he knew that I was coming, and he was expecting me. I asked him to please elaborate. He requested that I first explain my situation to him, and I did just that. After listening to my story, he confirmed that I was the man he was waiting on. The message he delivered today during his service seemed as if it was meant for me directly because it was. He instructed me to look at his notes on his desk. The title of the day's sermon was, "Superman is coming." I laughed, and told him I am no Superman.

The Bishop disagreed with me. He told me that I was Superman, and the problem is if I do not start to acknowledge my kryptonite, then it is going to continue to drain me. The alternative view he gave me on that day changed my life. He basically explained the life of the fictional character, Superman, and related it to my situation. Superman and I both were born as an innocent baby. We were born into a world of chaos. Superman was born during a time of war taking place on his planet, and I was born into a world of sin to fight a war of my own against Satan and all his temptations. Superman's parents lost the war, and his planet was destroyed. Before the war ended, they placed him into a spacecraft that would carry him to place he had never been before called Earth. The consequences of the battles we face and lose everyday tend to carry us to places we never thought we would see as well.

Superman was given super powers which made him practically unstoppable. We are also given powers that we call talents, and we can do all things through Christ who strengthens us, which makes us practically unstoppable as well. However, Superman was only weakened when faced with his kryptonite. Kryptonite is a crystalline substance created from the remains of his planet that was destroyed. I was clueless to the point he was trying to convey, and this is when he converted the story into an alternative view that allowed me to comprehend a concept that otherwise may have been hard to receive and even accept at the time. He explained that these crystal-like rocks were pieces of Superman's planet that fell upon the Earth after its destruction. They were, in effect, pieces of his past. Theoretically, Superman is drained of his powers whenever he is faced with pieces of his past.

That hit the nail on the head for me. I had no idea how much control my past had over me mentally that was hindering me from being productive. Things that happened in my childhood with my parents that I was not quite ready to let go of were hindering me. There were so many things I wish I had done differently in the past that I was constantly beating myself up over. That day, Bishop helped me see that if I was to renew my strength, I had to relinquish that control and let go of my troubled past. The forgiveness of those who hurt me is not for them; it's for me. This was not the first time that I was told that I needed to let go of my past, but that is easier said than done. However, if it was not for this alternative view that presented me with a different perspective that pinpointed my kryptonite at the time, I could still be oblivious to what was draining the life out of me, rendering me powerless. The new perspective altered my behavior, which allowed me to make better decisions, and I was able to change my situation. It wasn't that I needed to forget or pretend my past never existed; I simply needed to distance myself from it to avoid the effects of it. Once I accomplished this, I gained the strength to be productive and fight my way to a better future. I attended that church every week from that day on. As far as that thank you card I bought for my pastor, I returned to my previous church three months later and gave it to him. I attempted to explain the delay in delivering it. He stopped me and told me that it was ok because when someone does something for you out the kindness of their heart, they don't need thanks. Which taught me another valuable lesson, that we are blessed to be a blessing.

A Woman's Value

Men, how do we determine a woman's value? I do not think I would be out of line when I say as a man I believe that we determine a women's value starting from the outside, and then we may or may not even bother to work our way inward. This is sad when you think about it because women are so much more than their physical appearance. Oftentimes, men overlook the substance of a woman because of a beautiful smile or a few curves in her shape. We live in a world where the intelligence of a woman is second to her physical appearance. This is proven especially in the workplace dominated by men who try to determine the success of a woman based upon her looks alone. I can say that statement with certainty because I was guilty of this poor way of evaluating women for a position of employment.

In 2014, I was an office manager for a direct marketing firm. I worked alongside one other gentlemen who shared this same poor judgement of evaluating women for positions of employment. We shared an equal role in the hiring and interviewing processes. When evaluating the men, we were tough. We would look for the strongest candidate. We would thoroughly read over their résumés and take a close look at their qualifications and decide whether to bring the candidates in for an interview. The interview was even tougher. We drilled the male candidates looking for an individual with a strong personality and the ability to handle public speaking. The opportunity was door-to-door sales, and you must be fearless to excel at this position. The women, on the other hand, just had to be attractive. We would look at each other in agreement about her physical appearance and hire her. The hardest part was deciding whether she was going to train under my team or his team.

This was a terrible way of qualifying a woman for any position. These women may have been hired for their looks, but most turned out to be great hires and surprisingly excelled at the position and outshone several of the men we considered strong candidates. They may have interviewed in heels, but when it was time to hit the streets door-to-door, these women were all business. They tied up their sneakers and used that charm on the doorsteps of each house and did well. The male or female candidates must be extremely confident in their abilities to work a position that is 100% commission in the elements. These employees worked in the heat, cold, and rainy weather and knocked on complete strangers' doors attempting to sell them services they did not acquire about.

It goes without saying that women are so much more than just a pretty face and should not be hired strictly based off their physical appearance especially when they turned out to be of extreme value to the company. They were a joy to train and more coachable than the men. Most men felt as if they knew everything already and didn't require training. If I could do it all over again, the only thing I would do differently would be to hire more women. However, this does makes me wonder how many other company's men in positions of power make poor evaluation decisions like this and may not be as lucky as we were to hire the women based off their looks who still made significant contributions to the company. I am sure that hiring a beautiful woman who is not a good fit for a position can be costly for the company.

As I started my spiritual journey and began to acknowledge the true value of a woman, I gained a completely different perspective about placing women on a pedestal. "Why would I do that?" I asked. My spirit responded, "The reason is because she is a woman!" That was all the answer I needed, and it made complete sense to me. All the many reasons that make a woman who she is including the good and the bad represent why she is deserving of a spot on that pedestal. As I sat back a reflected on that statement, I thought of the four most important women in my life: my wife, my mother, my mother-in-law and my baby sister. I place each woman on her own pedestal. The love and respect I have for each of them differs from one to the other, but without question, they are the queens of my life.

This is where the conflict comes in. Why do men treat women so badly? Why do they disrespect them and hurt them? We all have important women in our life starting with our mothers whom we love so dearly. After marriage, the hierarchy order will change, but I am positive that all men can agree on a few things; we value our mother because she is a queen, and she deserves love and respect from everyone around her. No one is to hurt our mother, and no one is to ever disrespect her, or there will be consequences to pay. If I asked a group of men, "If you could afford it, what would be one thing you would love to do?," the answer would be to place their mothers in a better situation. It all started when we were younger. If I asked a group of young boys, "What would buy if you won one million dollars?," the very first thing a good percentage of them would say would be to buy their mother a house. In grade school, how many fights were started because a kid talked about somebody's mother?

Regardless of who she is, no woman can replace our mother. I think about how much we value our mother, so I ask the questions; "Are the women with whom we involve ourselves less of a woman than our mother?? Are they a different form of a woman than our mother?" No! I did not think so! Why are we so bad to them? These women are mothers and sisters too. They are deserving of the same love and respect. One wise saying suggests that the way a man treats his mother is the way he will treat his lady. Well, l that is an untrue statement. Many men praise their mother but walk all over their lovers. I believe the statement should read, "The man who loves his mother should know how to love and respect a woman and acknowledge her value."

Here is the alternative view; a man could never match the strength of a woman. There is nothing that a man can do that a woman cannot. Women can do any and everything a man can do. Even though it may not be as fast or efficient, she can do it. However, there is one thing that a woman can do that a man cannot do no matter how much money he has and no matter what his educational background may be. Only a woman can give birth! Speaking of that task, I would like to use the military for an example. The commanders in charge want to delegate the most challenging and important tasks to their strongest, most qualified soldiers. The reason for this is because they know that they can trust them to handle such a huge responsibility. Hypothetically, if men and women were soldiers in God's Army, He chose His more qualified soldier to handle such a huge responsibility like bringing all of us in this word.

We serve a God who can do all things, so giving that task to a man was an option. He gave men dominion over everything else, and regardless of the reason, He decided to let women handle the responsibility of repopulating the Earth. His move shows magnificent value in the likes of a woman. Giving birth to a child can be scary, extremely painful, and even life threatening, so if it was not for the selfless actions of a woman, the Earth would die out. There is no way a man can repay a woman for what she does on that birthing table, and if the Almighty God values women that much to honor them with task of bringing a beautiful life into this world, men, we are in no position to try to devalue them.

I also wonder how women determine their own value these days. Society is so hard on them. How do you deal with the judgment and the pressure and the standards oftentimes set by someone other than yourself? It seems almost impossible to be a woman in this world. Everywhere you turn, something or some-one is telling you how or what you should be. So many men tell you that your best is not good enough. Your friends make you feel like you are not smart enough. We have commercials implying you're not fit enough and music videos telling you what sexy should be. How do you determine your value? When you see all these woman with all these modifications, and you are watching reality TV showing you what reality should be, it all just seems so exhausting.

Well, please allow me to give you an alternative view. The best way I can I put this is you are perfect just the way you are. Yes! I know everyone says no one is perfect: however understand this, you were perfectly made by a perfect Creator who does not make mistakes. He made you in His perfect image. Ladies, wrap your mind around this when the man that God wants you to be with finds you. In His eyes, all He will see is perfection, flaws and all. So, any man who tells you anything other than you are perfect is, in fact, imperfect for you. Perfect is possible; you just must start by seeing the perfection within yourself.

Put Her Back

Take a trip with me down memory lane. Try to remember dating before you knew what dating really meant. I am talking about your middle school days when life was less complicated. I know you are probably wondering why I suggested middle school. Well, at that age, we had no clue what dating was supposed to be. I only knew that if I liked a girl I wanted her to like me back, and if she did, we would get into a relationship. In middle school, I had several short-term relationships. Some lasted only days, and I moved on to the next. I am sure a lot of you did the same. The point is as a child we did not hold on and tolerate a relationship we were unhappy with.

In middle school, I had a best friend named Ron. Our 7th grade year, I had a crush on one of the prettiest and smartest girls in our class. Ron was currently dating the best friend of the young lady whom I really liked. He told his girlfriend of my interest in her friend, and she put in a good word on my behalf. Before I knew it, I had a new girlfriend. Things started to change when Ron noticed a few differences in me that affected our friendship. It was mostly because I started to avoid him. My girlfriend chose some harsh words when speaking to me regarding Ron and his behavior in school. The last thing I wanted her to know was we were one in the same. I felt if she knew the real me, she would lose interest. In my mind, I was dating a young lady who was out of my league. I can recall telling myself, "Don't mess this up by being you." I felt like I needed to be more like her. I began to focus more, and my conduct was much improved. My girlfriend was extremely happy with the changes I made, and she made that very clear to me. However, I was putting a lot of pressure on myself to be pleasing in her eyes. I felt like if I was to keep her happy, I could never be myself. I wanted to walk and talk differently. I even wanted to dress differently, and as a 13-year-old boy, this was overwhelming and exhausting.

As a middle schooler in the 90's, the cool thing to do was to use profanity, and boy did Ron and I use a lot of it! Coincidentally, that was the number 1 thing my girlfriend stated she disliked the most about Ron. I made a conscious effort to ensure I limited my use of profanity. I found myself in a heated argument with Ron in the cafeteria after implying that he curses too much, and I think he used every curse word in the book in his response to that statement. He also had a few choice words of his own regarding my relationship. I vividly remember having that conversation with Ron. He looked me in the face and said, "I do not even know who you are anymore." My response was, "Well, maybe I am not the same person." I couldn't believe his next statement. He had the nerve to say, "Man, a dummy acting smart is an even bigger dummy!" All I could say was, "I am no dummy!" with a smile on my face. My friend said, "Just be yourself, dummy, and if she doesn't like it, that's ok. Just put her back because there are so many pretty fish in the sea."

To a 13-year-old boy with a crush, that statement sounded ridiculous, but shortly afterwards, I decided to end the relationship. Once I became a young adult, I realized that my friend gave me some good advice that day. It was a hard decision, but I had to face the clear fact that this young lady was a good thing, but that didn't mean that she was my good thing, and the best thing for me to do was respectfully put her back. As I take a closer look, by telling me to continue to be a dummy, he was basically telling me to stop trying to be someone that I am not and just to be myself. If that's not good enough, then it is acceptable to move on because there are other girls out there. Now, may I be clear? Growth in a relationship is good and often necessary, but understand there is a difference. Growth is a form of change, but growth does not change form. Allow me to elaborate; in a relationship, you should not need to change so much you lose sight of who you are.

Have you ever been in a relationship with a person who wanted to change everything about you, and no matter how much effort you put in to make those changes, it still was not enough? Well, the irony of it all was that person was not truly looking for you to change. Unknowingly, they were looking for someone else in you. A lot of us get that confused with growth. Well, by definition, growth is the process of developing or maturing physically, mentally, or spiritually; whereas, the definition of change is to make different entirely or transform. I believe it is safe to say that we should no longer try to change or change for someone; the goal should be to help each other grow.

I feel like we all have been in a similar situation at one point in which we force a relationship with someone who we were really into because we did not want to let them go for one reason for another. Coming from a man's standpoint, we are possessive, territorial, and just flat out selfish. We cannot handle the idea of that woman being with another man. In many cases, we are fully aware that we are no good for each other, and the relationship can even be considered toxic, yet we still hold on. The act of being selfish, is the only explanation. Women, on the other hand, tend to label that as "Love" and try to hold on and make it work even though it pains them to hold on. I belive at one point or another, women were convinced that holding on is a sure way of displaying love. I don't mean to burst your bubble, but that is not love. Love is kind and caring, and most importantly, love is a level of compatibility. Love is not a fist fight, and it does not argue, yell, and tear you down, but everyone argues, right? Wrong! Do not let that be an excuse; an argument filled with anger and belittling words versus a disagreement followed by effective communication are two different things.

So, if you are in a relationship full of problems and issues, and you two argue all the time, and no matter how hard you try you cannot seem to communicate with the other person, then it is very possible that you two are not compatible. We really do ourselves a disservice by staying in these types of relationships. We endure all these issues and problems and call it love. We tolerate so much and believe we are proving that love when we attempt to "make it work". Well, that is impossible. Compatibility is vital to a successful relationship. I am sure you can think of a past relationship in which you gave all that you could possibly give to make it work, and for some reason, it still wasn't good enough. This was exhausting and frustrating, right? Well, it wasn't your fault. There was nothing you could have done differently besides acknowledge that you were not compatible and realize that it was not your job to try to "make it work." Do you believe that? Well, we serve a God who is a Maker and Creator. He made you and created someone for you, which means that if you are with the right person, the work has already been done.

Compatibility, by definition, is a state in which two things can exist without problems or issue. Take notice that it did not say disagreements because disagreements are inevitable. No two people will ever agree on everything. However, here is what you should really understand. If those same two people are truly compatible, then the disagreements will not become problems. It is imperative for a man to understand that he must be fully compatible with a woman before pursuing any type of future with her, or he will surely fail her by wasting valuable time that cannot be returned, and by doing so, he hinders both their progress towards receiving true happiness. Her husband cannot find her if she is unavailable because she is involved with a man God never ordained for her to be with. God will not allow him to cross paths with his wife if he is holding on to another man's wife.

As a man, I can say that after spending time with a woman, we know if we are truly compatible with her or not. The problem is most of us realize that we are not, and instead of respectfully putting her back, we ignore it and decide to just hold on to her and place her on our team, so to say, with no plans of seriously being with her. Why? Because we are selfish! She may be gorgeous, and we are not selfless enough to walk away from her. This is a problem which should be an easy fix. If more men had higher aspirations for the happiness of a woman regardless of how they feel when they realize that she is not the one for them, they would put her back.

Ladies, this goes for you too. Put yourself back. In most cases, you realize sooner than a man does that you two are not compatible. You acknowledge that God did not send you this man and have the nerve to say, "God, I know this is not my husband." Yet you still give him your time. Why? So many women acknowledge that they can have any man that they want, and this a factual statement. Why don't they want the man they deserve? This, I do not understand. If you can have the man you deserve, if only you firmly desired him and only him, why would you hold on to a man with whom you are not compatible and who hurts and disrespects you?

Here is a little analogy to help us picture the consequences of ignoring the bad signs early on in a relationship and holding on. Look it this way; the car crashes that happen on the highways at high rates of speed are extremely bad in some cases. The cars are crushed like soda cans, and if people were to guess, they would be sure that the outcome for the people inside was fatal. However, in many of these cases, the passengers walk away without a scratch. This is symbolic to life moving fast. Things are going to happen, but God has us covered, and in spite of how fast life happens, He has the ability to keep his covering over you. However, a lot of car accidents occur on city streets at decreased speeds when people run red lights or ignore stop signs. People are left with life changing injuries that they must live with for the rest of their lives. This is symbolic to you dealing with a man, and you decide to ignore all bad signs from God. You guys will crash, and you will have to live with the damages he caused for the rest of your life. If you understand that when signs are ignored, people crash, why do you continue to take such a risk? Allow me to guess...because you love him? Well, why don't you try loving yourself more? When you decide to do this, the blinders will come off, and you will see clearly that you do not deserve what he put you through. Moreover, you will see that it is well worth walking away from that situation because there is a man out there looking for you, and he is equipped with the tools needed to love you the right way, and he can help you forget that you have ever been hurt.

This decision for a man to put a woman back is easier said than done, it requires a man to place the woman's happiness above his own. The harsh reality of a woman to walking away from a man that's undeserving of her is extremely difficult, especially for a woman in a situation that seems to be the norm. She knows other woman who have been through what she is experiencing, so she's content because at least she knows what she can expect. I do not believe women are afraid of something better. It is the possibility of something worse that has her fearful, and fear stops progression.

Allow me to give you an alternative view as I look closer at the word *fear*, which is a very unpleasant emotion. Faith is complete trust, and we all have heard that fear contradicts faith both to whom we have control over and the power of choice between the two. Fear is caused by the belief that something or someone is dangerous, and trust is a firm belief in something or someone. The Bible tells us to believe in God and all His goodness. Whereas, your fears tell you to believe in yourself and operate in your fears. If God did not give you the spirit of fear, then in whom would you say your trust lies...God or yourself? Someone once told me that our ears were placed purposely on the outside of our face because we were not meant to listen to ourselves, ponder on that for a second!

Ladies, when deciding if you should hold onto another person or put him or her back, ask yourself is this relationship pleasing to God? If not, operate fearlessly in your faith, and God will order your steps. I challenge you all to choose wisely. Your belief is your acceptance and to believe in a perfect God that doesn't make mistake, is to accept that perfect is possible.

The Perfect Person Is Possible

How is it possible that we were made in such a perfect image by such a perfect Creator, but we live in a world where nobody is perfect? How many times have you been told or even said to someone else, "If you are looking for somebody perfect, that person does not exist"? Well, I beg to differ. You learned in Chapter One that you are perfect, so that eliminates the possibility of nobody being perfect, right? In spite of your flaws, seeing perfection in yourself will help you see the perfection in others. Most of us are led to believe that we all were made imperfect without having a true understanding exactly what that statement means. You soon will see that we are all imperfect, which is the direct opposite of the word, perfect. This is the main reason why finding the perfect person is possible.

To think that material things can be perfect, but people cannot be perfect kind of confuses me. How is it possible to believe that with the proper amount of time we can find the perfect item, but the search for the perfect person is impossible? Just like that, we may have just discovered the actual problem. If we pursued our spouses patiently and subjectively the way we pursue the perfect materialistic item, we may surprise ourselves. When searching for things that we want, we tend to be more patient, and if it is not perfect, we will pass on it. We try our best not to settle when spending money on things that we want. We look for perfection all the time, which is why it takes us so long at the grocery store. It takes a while to pick something as simple as a carton of eggs or a bag of bread.

Why don't we just grab the first one we see and take it home? Well, for starters the eggs may have been mishandled or dropped, and now, they are all cracked up, or the bread may have been smashed. We inspect these items closely and if they are is not to our liking, we put them back and continue to look until we find some that are. We may even decide to drive clear across town to look elsewhere, and in spite of the drive we do not settle there either, we often decided to wait to prevent from purchasing a subpar item. When dating it seems as if we value our time differently, the decision and time put in to drive across town, is the reason why subpar is unacceptable. When dating, the decision to settle for a subpar, is due to all the effort and time we put in. How many people do you know that feels, they have giving a person so much of their time, it has to work? The fact of the matter is, your time is only wasted, when you realized how you've settled.

As a car salesman, I assist anywhere from 5 to 20 people a day from all different walks of life with different financial situations. The one thing they all have in common is that they all are looking for a good deal on the perfect car. These consumers are unlike most people. They do their research sometimes for months. They request the Carfax, which is the vehicle history report. Some people may search dealership to dealership looking for this perfect car before stepping foot on the lot. Once the consumer narrows down the vehicle search and locates the automobile, the mission to find the perfect car has only just begun.

Upon arrival at the car dealership, the consumer will see that there are many models alike lined up next to each other. At this time, you would think the consumer would choose the very first one he or she sees and buy it? That would be a sales professional's dream, but unfortunately, it does not happen that way. Granted, this is the exact model the consumer is looking for, and it looks nice. So, what is the problem? Well, the fact of the matter is the appearance only plays a small role in finding the perfect car. Now, most people like to think it is the test drive that is the most important aspect of buying a new car, but that is not true. Most similar models will drive pretty much the same; however, it is the specs on the inside of the vehicle that sell it to the customer. The customer is most interested to see if the vehicle comes equipped with all the features that the he or she finds to be important.

Many people are interested in how the car feels when they sit in it. You will not believe how many people come to the dealership only to complete the sitting test during which they will go from model to model, and all they would like to do is sit in the vehicle. Now, earlier on in my career as a sales professional, I could not understand this for the life of me, but the fact of the matter is that it is imperative that the consumer chooses carefully because this is a huge investment. The customer needs to be allowed to spend time sitting in the vehicle because it is a critical part of the purchasing process. The concept of sitting in the vehicle allows the consumer the time to allow the vehicle to speak to them. From a religious standpoint, the customer allows God to send the confirmation they need to be sure this is the right vehicle.

Why is it that in our pursuit of a mate, we don't treat our investment the same? Are we not investing so much more time and money that cannot be returned if we waste it? Most of us are not patient at all when it comes choosing the right person to give your time, and you wonder why you seem to always end up with someone equivalent to the broken eggs or the smashed bread. To make matters worse, you actually convinced yourself of this awful decision because you then believed you had the ability to fix this person, and when you realized that this task was never yours to take on, it was a little too late. You were too invested to turn back, so you were forced to "make it work"!

Imagine this, if the next person you were interested in told you that they did a full background check on you, how would you feel? Most people would feel awkward and may even be turned off, and it is very safe to say that there are some people would be offended by the idea. Why would they be offended? Are we not allowed to do our research on people before giving them our time?

In today's society, men and women equally are all about the test drive. This correlates to our sexual behavior which makes it acceptable to look at sex as a trial period. Well, if you hop behind the wheel of a car without doing you research, and the engine blows up, you cannot blame anyone but yourself for the pain.

The secret is before you test drive or allow yourself to be test driven, you should do the sitting test. Allow yourself a moment for that voice to speak to you and give you the conformation you need before this test drive leaves tire marks on your life. Ladies, a real man does not need a test drive if he has a relationship with your Maker because he can rest assured you have been manufactured to perfection.

In our pursuit of people, we are almost expected to act impulsively. We live in a society of people who are so in fear of wasting time that we waste time. Allow me to elaborate. We have already discovered that as a people we have no patience when it comes to choosing the right person. We, furthermore, support that statement by presenting the question, "Are we doing this or not?" Again, no one has time to waste, but by operating this way, you waste so much more time. This way is kind of a head-first mentality in which we rush into something headfirst without much thought. All we know is we kind of like this person, and then we are kicking ourselves 6 months later because of all the time we just wasted.

The main issue behind this method is it then sends us into an ongoing cycle because we justify our previous decision by saying, "You live, and you learn." That's right. We pat ourselves on the back as we explain to other people just how much we have learned from that last 6 months of turmoil. Eventually, we find ourselves attempting to justify these bad decisions by calling them growth because we allegedly learned a lot from the heartache. It pains me to think that as a people we believe we must go through the fire to understand that we can get burned. We serve a God who loves us so much that He gave His only begotten Son for us. Do you really believe your Father in Heaven wants you to endure all the pain you have felt in your lifetime to learn the small lessons you had to learn the hard way? Allow me to answer that. No! He does not because He is a part of you. When you hurt, God feels pain too.

God gives us free will, which is the ability to act at our own discretion. This means that in every situation in your life, you were presented with a choice, and the choice you made led to a time of pain. From that pain, you learned a valuable lesson. However, do not think for one minute you had to go through the pain to learn the lesson. Look closer at our justification of bad choices, "You live, and you learn," To me, when you shrug off a horrible decision and use this phrase, you are telling yourself is ok to live recklessly because you will learn from it, right? This would only be partially true if we learned from our mistakes, or better yet, if we applied what we learned, but a lot of us continue to do the same things over and over and expect different results which is the definition of insanity. By reading this book, you are already doing the direct opposite of what that phrase is telling you to do by honoring what God would prefer we do.

The Bible gives us a pretty good blueprint, a form of direction, and a list of commandments that are designed to help mold your decision making and the way you should live. You were taught to read the Bible since you were a kid, so in all honesty, we have the phrase all backwards. We should "learn and then live." Can you imagine the impact this would have in the world on relationships especially if we turned this around? If he took the time to learn how to treat you first or if you learned truly how bad his temper was beforehand, would you have made a different choice? What would your choices be if you both learned that you two were not compatible before the arguments and bad break-ups? Would you say things may have been different?

Learning and then living is essential to finding that perfect person. You still do not believe that perfect is possible? It is so easy to be content and just settle for an undeserving person due the fact that we believe that perfect is not possible. We have hard time seeing perfection in ourselves. All we know is our flaws and imperfections, and I agree that we are all imperfect, but that is the key. Our imperfections are what makes perfect possible. The definition of the word, *imperfect*, is "not perfect, faulty or incomplete."

The Bible says that a woman was created from a man's rib, and if you think about a rib cage with a rib missing, that is a sense of incompletion. That should tell you several things. For starters, ladies, you are the prize and not the other way around. A man who thinks that he is complete without a woman is not yet a man. It tells me as a man that each woman in the world is an individual rib, and they come in all shapes and sizes. A man must take his time and be selective and find his rib that will fit his cage perfectly. If you notice, the text says "his" rib meaning not just any rib no matter how good the rib looks. His rib cage is theoretically shaped in a certain way, so if he finds the woman that God want him to be with, she may not be perfect in the eyes of anyone else, but she will be a perfect fit for him. His strengths will be her weaknesses and her strengths his weaknesses.

This is the reason why in a relationship we cannot "make it work" because it is impossible for us to change the shape of that rib and force it to fit his cage. If you force it, something is going to break. The fact of the matter is there is no way possible for you to make a relationship work that God has not ordained. My mother once told me to seek God's plan because the quickest way to make God laugh is to tell Him what you got planned.

Men, what does this mean to you? It means you are in a world full of ribs, but only one of them is yours. It is your job to find it. The proper way to do this is gather one up, take your time, and pray about it. Don't misuse it because the moment you receive the notion from God that this is not yours, you are to put it back. Ladies, what does this mean to you? It means your husband is actively trying to find you. Do not allow yourself to be held by a man who knows that you are not his rib. Put yourself back. Ladies, remember you are a good thing but just not any man's good thing.

To your husband, you are a gift, and for God to allow a man to receive this gift, he must be right with Him first. However, even If he is right with God, He will not send him to find you if you are unavailable. The misconception is that God will send this man to save you. I am sorry, but God does not operate this way. He loves that man equally, so He will not send him into your world of chaos. Yes, even though you been praying for God to change your situation and send you a man, a man will come alright, but I ensure you he wasn't sent by God. Don't be fooled.

The first thing to do is make the choice to allow God to enter your life. Welcome Him into your relationship and put Him first. Pray a little differently understanding that He loves you, so He does not change your situation; He changes you. Pray and allow Him to change your heart, and then, ultimately, you will change your situation by making better decisions, putting God first in everything that you do and allowing yourself to be put back or having the strength to put yourself back.

At this point in your life, you will understand your value clearly and place it above the needs of any man, and by loving yourself and embracing your singleness, you will never feel alone again. God is with you, and you are now available for your husband, and he is coming. Just stay in your castle and wait!!

Stay in Your Castle

Would you agree that it is hard for a woman to find a good man? I have heard women say this for as long as I can remember, but why exactly is that? I searched the internet, and I found a few answers to this question. I would like to take a little time to disagree with all of them. The first reason I found why it is so hard for a woman to find a good man is because of society. There is a lack of good men because of the change in society, and they do not make men like they used to make them. Well, unless there is something going on that I do not know about, I think the making process is still the same. A man and a woman decide to lay down together, and well, I don't think I have to go into detail, but the point is we still make them the same. I believe in our society today, both men and women are making decisions without realizing that the choices they make affect the actions of the opposite sex. A woman has complete control over how a man pursues her, the decisions she make send messages for him to respond to. The question is; are you making decisions that directly coordinates with your happiness or his? Ladies, making the decisions that coordinate with your true happiness, poses a question for him. He then has to decide whether to adhere and make you happy or decide against it and deal with the consequences. If he decides against the decisions you made for your happiness, these are the signs that you are not to ignore and put yourself back. Do not be afraid to operate in your happiness and only yours, especially in the beginning of a relationship, because the decisions made in the likes your happiness do not sacrifice his, for making you happy should make him happy.

When I reference "Grass", I mean women. Another reason I found in my research was that it was hard for a woman to find a good man because men are always holding out for something better. They are always looking for greener grass. I agree with this statement. Most men are looking for the softer, greener grass a big portion of the time. However, whose fault is this? Ladies, the decisions you make for yourself will dictate the level of respect that man has for that grass. Why would you allow a man to even step foot on grass that he has not fertilized and watered? If he doesn't care about the maintenance and attention this grass needs to be beautiful, then it's obvious that he is not concerned with the growth of the grass, and he plans to just walk all over it.

Ladies, understand men love to cut their "own" grass, which means your first decision is to require him to make it his before he touches it. Men, take pride in being that guy with the prettiest lawn in the neighborhood. If you are going to allow a man into your yard, demand that he make it his top priority and put in the effort in that it takes to ensure that this is the greenest grass around. Without sunshine, the grass will surely die, so if you allow a man to be a dark cloud over your grass, don't be surprised when he damages it and moves on. A lot of people, in general, just do not take care of things that are not theirs, so if he is not willing to make it his, then he does not deserve to even touch it.

One of the most common reasons I found in my search that a good man is so hard to find is most of these men today are not ready for a committed relationship, and all they want to do is have sex. Now, honestly, ladies, a man can only do what you allow him to do, so I believe there are some questions that need to be answered. Why is getting sex from a woman so easy these days? When did women become so willing to have sex? The answer to those two questions will explain why a lot of these men are only focused on sex. How many times have you heard someone say it was just sex? Who changed the meaning behind sex? I don't know the percentage of meaningless sexual encounters that men and women engage in today, but I am willing to bet you that it is high. If a woman is willing to allow a man to enjoy the most precious parts of her without demanding that he earn it, how can she then expect him to put in the work required for it to be anything more than sex?

Take a moment and imagine all the things you must endure on your job. Now, imagine if your employer paid you your entire salary up front for the year and then expected you to continue to come to work on time, full of energy with a smile. Could you do it? Now, be honest! Of course not! None of us could continue to hold our tongue and endure all that we do on the job day in and day out if we have already been compensated. Well, essentially, this is what you are asking of a man when you allow him to enjoy such a beautiful payday before he puts in the work.

Some women feel like sex is all they have to offer because of the changes in society and the way in which living has evolved. Granted, one person cannot change the world but understand that you can control your reality. If a serious and committed relationship is what you desire, then that is exactly what you deserve. Every man is very capable of being a good man. It just takes the right woman to bring it out of him. So instead of trying to figure out if he is the right man, ask yourself are you the right woman. The right woman is not like the others so be different. Require a man to pursue you subjectively and not objectively because objectively is, in a way, not influenced by personal feelings and subjectively is the direct opposite. This means you are not just a piece of meat, so you should not allow a man to treat you like one. If you do, then it is you who has set the tone of how that man will treat you moving forward.

The best thing about valuing yourself is having zero tolerance when it comes to being pursued the right way. It gives you a defense against the foolery of a man. It helps you filter out the guy or guys who are only looking to just play with your heart. If a guy is not truly ready for what you have decided you want for yourself, he will fall by the wayside so fast because your standards and requirements will be too high for him. Initially, he will try to get you to drop that guard of yours and ease up by telling you everything he thinks you want to hear.

At that time, you have a decision to make. Either lower your standards and trust what he says, or you can stand firm and stay true to yourself, and by doing so, you present him with a decision to either adhere to your terms and step up and be the man you need him to be or give up and move on. If he decides to move on, you have to understand and allow it. This is a blessing, and you have saved yourself a lot of time and prevented yourself from enduring the pain that would have come with you trying to make that work.

Another reason it is hard for a woman to find a good man is because a lot of these boys are not truly ready to step up and be a man. The problem runs much deeper than that. You may be dealing with a man-child, which is a real thing. You would think that the idea of an immature man who refuses to grow up would be the easiest reason for a woman to exit the relationship. Instead, many women think this is cute until they find out the hard way that they can't raise a man. Why does a woman take on this task? You always end up having to make excuse after excuse for him and do anything you can to take the load off his shoulders until you find yourself basically carrying him.

The problem with carrying a man is you find yourself chastising and nagging him all the time because he is not handling business the way a man should. You always must remind him of important dates and events. You find yourself frustrated and constantly disappointed when he does not follow through with anything he said he would do. You cannot communicate with him about how you are feeling because the last thing he wants to do is have an adult conversation or be held accountable, so he just finds a way to blame you so convincingly that you also blame yourself. Well, ladies, the good thing is you are one decision away from doing better because you all know you can do badly by yourself. The best thing you can do is make the hard decision to move on and allow him to be a kid. Losing you may be his motivation to grow up and become a better man, and if the opportunity presents itself in the future, he may be better suited for you. Timing is everything.

Now, allow me to give you an alternative view on why it is so hard for women to find a good man. It is not her job to find one! The Bible tells us about the man who finds a wife and not about him being found by one. It is not the job of any woman to get out and try to find a man. By doing so, she does nothing but make it harder for the man she desires to find her. The man who she deserves is actively looking for her, and if she does not stay put, she is making his search very difficult. I believe that all the reasons listed above are the true reasons why finding and being found is so difficult. It is those exact reasons that give women across the world a false reality, which makes them believe that they must take matters into their own hands and find a man.

The truth of the matter is women are queens, and queens are only required to do one thing, be a queen. Your prince charming is looking for you, and this should give you all the confidence you need to be patient. A prince cannot be a king until he finds his queen, so if you are not in the castle when he comes knocking on the door, how will he find you?

There is a fairy tale about a woman named Rapunzel. In this story, like all women around the world today, she was beautiful. She was born to a king and queen, which meant it was her birthright to be a queen. Like all women, Rapunzel yearned for love and her king. As the time went by, I am sure there was nothing more Rapunzel wanted to do besides take matters into her own hand to find her king. Rapunzel was forced to be patient and just look out a small window with a heart full of desires because she was locked away in a castle. It was impossible for Rapunzel physically to get out and find her king. Rapunzel was not only locked away in the castle, but also she was guarded by a dragon. Every knight in this fairy tale wanted to have Rapunzel as his queen, but the brave knights had a huge task ahead of them to prove themselves deserving of the beautiful Rapunzel. The deserving knight would have to rescue his queen from the castle, which required the slaying of her dragon first.

This task was not to be easy. Only the most equipped knight would prevail and have Rapunzel as his queen. The point is Rapunzel didn't have to do anything besides stay in the castle. Imagine if the brave knight took on this task and succeeded and got to the top the castle, and Rapunzel was not there because she was out trying to find a good knight. It is important for women of the world today to understand that is not your job to take matters into your own hands and find a man. The man that you deserve already has a hard-enough task trying to find you. The last thing you want to do is make his search harder.

When I say stay in your castle, I am simply saying stay true to yourself. Lock yourself away from all these undeserving men and save yourself a lot of time and heartache. As a woman, put yourself in the shoes of Rapunzel. In that story, every knight was trying to rescue Rapunzel and have her as his wife. All but one failed. Like the fairy tale, ladies, every man is trying to have you. That task should not be easily won. Rapunzel was guarded by a dragon. Ladies, everything you went through in your past that has hurt you and brought you insecurities, makes it difficult for you to trust. This is why your guard is up. Ladies, this your dragon. Require a man to slay him first. An ill-equipped man will not be able to handle nor understand your dragon. He will expect you to just trust him and drop your guard, which means slay your own dragon. Instead, this is when you feed the dragon and make him stronger because only the right man can slay your dragon. Stand firm. An undeserving man will view you as stuck up, and that is perfectly fine. If you are lucky, he will give up and move on.

The man who deserves you will tell you to keep your dragon for he understands it is his job to give you a reason to trust. The man who is fully equipped to slay your dragon will be patient with you, persistent, and consistent. At the same time, he will be symbolically slaying your dragon by not shying away from your skepticism. He will embrace it and let his actions speak louder than his words. Therefore, you two will live happily ever after.

The Taraji Henson Effect

There is a debatable perception that a lot of women have today which is that all men cheat; the problem with this is perception is reality. Your perception is what you believe. What you believe can alter your behavior, and your behavior can very well determine your reality. We must be careful because perception can often lie about the way things are especially if that perception is blurred by lies and misinformation. If this occurs, it is safe to say that your reality may need some revisions.

We can credit a lot the insecurities women have going into a relationship today to the perception that all men cheat. It has women failing to communicate and operating in fear due to the anticipation of the pain caused by unfaithfulness. However, the laws of cause and effect state that whatever you put out in the universe is typically what comes back. Your perception should be determined by your truths of what you see. Instead, a lot of what we believe today is due the truths of others. Many people would be opposed to admitting that they are a follower, but the reality is that a lot of our behaviors are determined by our peers. It is my perception that women cheat simply because men cheat. I believe this to be factual in reality. Women are known to be more faithful in relationships than men, and typically, if a woman is cheating, she is currently being cheated on. I truly believe that a man can cheat with little or no reason at all. However, I believe a woman would have to have emotional motivation to cheat on a man. I could be wrong, but that is my perception. I also believe that if any woman was to meet a man who was so laser-focused on her desires and treated her like the queen she is, that woman would not cheat on that man. Unlike the men I know with amazing women who give their all to the relationship, and they are still being cheated on.

For this reason, I understand the perception; however, ladies, it runs deeper than you think. It is important that you understand that this perception that every man cheats does not have to be your reality. The truth of the matter is all men do not cheat. Some realities are just harder to face than others. For example, it is very possible that you are being cheated on by a man whom you should not be with.

Allow me to give you an alternative view on why that man may be cheating on you because it has absolutely nothing to do with you and everything to do with him. He is cheating on you because you are not his Taraji Henson, and I am not saying that because you are not a celebrity. Trust me. That has nothing to do with it at all.

Taraji P. Henson is an award-winning actress and singer. I was introduced to Taraji in 2001 when she played in her first prominent role in the comedy-drama film, *Baby Boy*. That film was arguably one of the best movies at that time. She portrayed a character named Yvette. I instantly felt myself crushing on this beautiful woman. In the film, she played alongside Tyrese Gibson. I just remember being upset with Tyrese throughout the entire film. Jody, Yvette's boyfriend portrayed by Tyrese, was all but a perfect gentleman, which is very similar to the boys who call themselves men these days. In the film, Jody still lived at home with his mother. He did not have job or a car. He drove Yvette's car as if it was his own. Jody was a terrible boyfriend to Yvette. He cheated and lied to her repeatedly. Yvette was very similar to most women these days. She was employed and had her own vehicle and her own apartment. It appears that Yvette's only downfall was the baby boy she chose to love and the fact that she allowed him to hurt her time and time again.

There were a few key moments in the movie that really stood out to me. The scene when Jody went out to the strip club, and Yvette found out about it. Yvette was furious, but the only part of that conversation I remember was when she requested that he would not bring back any sexual diseases from one of the nasty girls. This statement was honestly disturbing for me because I wasn't sure if this meant that she accepted his behavior as long as he was careful not to bring anything home to her. The second moment for me in the movie was during another argument between the two, and as an attempt to get the truth out of him, she told him that she knew he was with other girls. She made it clear that she didn't like it. However, she knew this was a part of who he was. This statement that was hard for me to understand. My question to Yvette would be, "If you know these things, why you are still with him?" Now, Jody's moment of honesty really upset me when he looked her in her face and told her that she has his son, and she would probably be his wife one day. Probably? Now, that's hilarious. I could not believe he told her that he makes love to her and wants to be with her, but he also has sex with other women. In closing, he told her that's the situation and deal with it!

At the time, it was hard for even me to comprehend, but as I watched the movie, all I could think to myself was this beautiful woman does not deserve this. Why is she putting up with that? She is gorgeous. Doesn't she know she can do better? That's when it dawned on me that there are so many women today in similar situations with men who they have decided to give their hearts, and they deserve so much better. If only there was a way to articulate effectively to them in a way that would understand that there is no reason why they should hold on and allow themselves to be disrespected in this manner. This was a made-up character; however, I was sitting there feeling angered by the way she was being treated in this fictional relationship. I had the strongest desire to tell Yvette that she deserved better, and by "better," I meant me! Ladies, the reality of it all is there is a man out there who will notice your situation and acknowledge all your pain and suffering. He will then desire to dry up your tears, patch up your wounds, and shoulder all your insecurities. This man will help put the pieces of your broken heart back together patiently and make it his life's goal to ensure that you never feel that way again. Most importantly, he will make you forget what it felt like to be treated that way.

I became mentally intrigued with Taraji. As a result, it altered my mentality as man by enhancing my desires to want to be good to her. I can recall conversing with my buddies at that time. I was asked hypothetically if I was in a relationship with Taraji would I cheat on her. It's as if I was appalled by the question. Without a doubt or bit of hesitation, my answer was a firm, "No!" I did not know Taraji at all and had no clue what type of woman she was or whether or not she was good for me. However, the point is I felt and desired her mentally. I could say with confidence that I believe that I would not have the desire to cheat on her. Again, this effect has nothing to with Taraji being a celebrity because it is very possible that the right man will desire you in the same manner, and you can expect not to be cheated on.

So, ladies, understand that there is nothing wrong with you if you are being cheated on. It is very possible that he is not as mentally intrigued with you as I was with Taraji, which means you do not have the Taraji effect on him that would alter his desire to cheat on you. Look at it this way. It was my perception, which means I believed that I would not have the desire to cheat on Taraji, and if my beliefs have the power to alter my behavior, then it is very possible to make this idea of not cheating on her my reality.

It is safe to say I became a fan of Taraji. So, my question is, ladies, would you say that your man is a fan of yours? How does he feel about you mentally? Being cheating on has nothing to do with you but everything to do with him. My godmother's husband is her number one fan. He praises the ground that she walks on, and to this day, he will tell anyone that he talks to about her. That is one reason their relationship is as beautiful as it is. She is amazing, and he works extremely hard to make sure he continues to deserve her. He once told me that he deserves her, but she doesn't deserve him. I did not know what that meant. He simply told me that's just the way he looks at his life. He loves himself and believes he deserves an amazing woman, and he has her. However, his wife is so amazing she deserves better than him. She deserves the world. Unfortunately, it's not his to give, but he will spend the rest of his life trying to give it to her. He helped me understand that they are equal, so it's not that he feels inadequate or that he is beneath his wife. It's how he feels about her mentally that makes him believe she deserves more than he can give, and for that, he will forever strive to give her the best of him. It's extremely hard to cheat on a woman if you are too busy trying to give her the world.

We Are on the Same Team

The title is the most interesting component of a relationship. How is it that we can date a person carefree with no "title" and enjoy the relationship so much it makes us want to title it officially? The moment we do the carefree enjoyment goes away, and we jump right into possessive micromanaging mode as if relationships are not complicated enough. I believe we contribute a lot of the complication ourselves. One of main reasons why relationships are so complicated is due to the lack of trust, and I do not mean broken trust in the relationship after something has happened. I mean trust from the very beginning after we stamp and title it. It may stem from events in our past, but we do not realize how detrimental this lack of trust is to our relationship goals. We are so fearful of being cheated on we try to micromanage the relationship to ensure it doesn't happen. The perception that everybody cheats has us expecting the person to be deceitful. As a result, we check emails and phones looking for something negative. A lot of us are so distrusting it is hard for us to realize that we are self-sabotaging as if we prefer to look for the negatives and hurt ourselves rather than trust that person and be happy with the positive aspects about that person.

I've spoken with quite a few people who confirm this by telling me that they prefer to search for negativity and deal with the pain at that moment rather than be "naive" and trust someone who may end up hurting them much later. My question is, "Why would you be with that person who you fear will eventually hurt you?" This is preventable. End that relationship now! It is a true statement that if you look for something long enough you are bound to find it, but understand it's also true that what you do not know cannot hurt you. As far as being naïve, I challenge you to exercise your faith and give that relationship to God. It is possible for you to live in the peace of not searching for negativity and enjoy the happiness of being oblivious to anything in that relationship that is not pleasing to you.

The key is understanding that you are not obligated to be hurt. God can remove you from that relationship peacefully. Imagine waking up one day and God placed it on your heart that relationship is not going in the direction that you desire, so you effectively communicate that, and you both decide to end as friends. You never find out about the negativity of what really was going on, which means you were never hurt by it, and yet you are out of that relationship in peace. Leaving a relationship on such a positive note allows you to leave with all the positive lessons you've learned from it, which makes you mentally available for God to cover your next relationship and make it your best. I don't know when we developed the false idea that we only learn from the negative things that occur in relationships. It does not always have to be something negative that kills a relationship; it is possible that couple may not have been compatible. That is not a negative thing at all especially when the lesson learned is positive.

Trust is so important in a relationship. When you chose one to be person to be with out of the billions of people in the world, you must trust them. Trust them, trust your decision, but most importantly trust God. You have to have faith in your relationship because there is no way you can control or prevent another adult from making any decision he or she wants to make. Despite how much you monitor their whereabouts, check their emails, or go through their cell phone, you cannot control adults. You are only guaranteed to be stressed out by looking for something that may or may not exist and cause conflict in your relationship.

The last thing we want in our relationship is conflict. We must be on one accord. We on the same team, and a relationship between two people is like basketball teammates. In the game of basketball, there is a head coach. His job is to put players together on a team who are compatible and likeminded with the discipline to be obedient to his direction. He brings together players who are humble enough to be receptive to his correction and laser-focused on the execution of his plan of action to win as a team. The play book is drawn up by the head coach which consists of well-developed plays of actions that will prepare the players for the opposition. The opposition is looking to do whatever it takes to keep the team from winning. The head coach has carefully considered all the opposition's plans of attack, and he will coach the team play-by-play to ensure he always is one step ahead of the defense. The players must trust that there is no situation that the head coach has not seen and have absolute faith in his guidance and preparation to ensure their success.

There are arguably two positions in basketball that are vital to the team's ability to put up points and carry the team to a victory. Those two positions are the point guard and the shooting guard. The point guard is typically the primary position responsible for controlling the ball most of the time. He is the guy you may see handling the basketball as he makes his way up court. He has a very important job to be smart and protect the basketball always. The point guard gets his direction directly form the head coach, and he must communicate effectively with the other players and put the coach's plan into motion. He must be selfless to know when to make decisions that may not directly benefit him but benefit the entire team. The point guard must be a great leader to be in command and earn the trust of his teammates. He must trust and have faith in the ability of his teammates to play their position.

The shooting guard can be the primary position if needed but is mostly the secondary position that plays off the actions of the point guard. The shooting guard helps the point guard in several ways and can even carry the load if the point guard needs to rest. In spite sharing an equal amount of responsibility to protect the ball, the shooting guard must be submissive enough to allow the point guard to lead. The two of them must be in sync mentally and communicate effectively always. They complement each other, neither can win alone. It is imperative that the shooting guard understands that in order to play the position successfully, there must absolute trust in the point guard's decision making and ability to lead with a full understanding that the job of the point guard is to place the team in the best position possible to be successful.

Both positions are responsible for communicating effectively at all times., Arguments and anger have no room on a team. Arguments amongst teammates cause frustration followed by pride, which is an unwanted distraction that will make it difficult to work as a team and execute the game plan. Effectively communicating through a small debate is normal. Teammates may have a difference of opinions. One may be seeing the court or the opposition from an angle than other teammates. Therefore, being receptive to others' feedback is important. It is Equally important for both to support, encourage, and uplift each other to heights neither thought they could reach.

Now, allow me to give you an alternative view. A relationship is very similar to the game of basketball. We also have a head coach. We are coached by the greatest Coach of all, and He wants us all to come together and be successful. His name is God. "Coach G" is what I like to call Him, and the Bible is His playbook. He has given us a blueprint of plans on how to play this game called life. He has carefully drawn up these plans we call His Commandments, and He has the opposition's every move in mind and wants to equip us with the tools we need to be successful. There is no situation that God has not seen. He created the game, and if we execute His plans, the enemy coming against us does not stand a chance. The major difference in coaching styles between a basketball coach and Coach G is that God isn't predicting what will happen next. He knows exactly what lies ahead, so having faith and trust in His direction should be easy.

The basketball signifies the relationship that must be cherished and protected always. The man is represented by the point guard. He should be the head of the relationship. His first obligation is to protect the relationship. He must handle it with care; if he does not and is dribbling the relationship any kind of way, the opposition will surely steal it from him. The woman is represented by the shooting guard who must be submissive enough to allow the man to lead because it is the man's job to ensure he always put his woman in the best position possible to be successful. In a relationship, it is imperative that both parties understand that we cannot win without absolute trust and faith in each person's ability to play the position they have been given in our game. If not, cut that player and recruit another because losing sucks.

In basketball, neither position can micromanage the other to be sure that that person is playing their position properly. The point guard must have a level of faith that the shooting guard is just as committed to the position as he is to his. If the point guard was dribbling the ball up the court and unfocused on his obligation of protecting the ball and he was too caught up in watching and dictating to the shooting guard what should and should not be done, instead of just trusting, the team would be ineffective. If the shooting guard was too busy to commit to the position because the focus is on what the point guard is doing wrong, when the play is called, the shooting guard would not be in the proper position to receive the ball, and in both cases, the defender will be right there to steal.

Arguments and fighting have no room in a relationship. Frustration and pride are the enemy's most used tool against us to destroy relationships. Just like basketball, the more frustrated a player gets on a team will surely affect his ability to perform on the level needed to win, and it will not be long until that player requests to be traded to another team where he feels appreciated. Coach G says anything of anger is not of him so be slow to your anger in your relationships. Disagreements are normal, but that does not mean we cannot communicate effectively and get our point across without offending or attacking the other person.

In a relationship, we are supposed to be on the same team with the same goal in mind. If you are going recruit someone to play on your team, trust them to play the position to the best of their ability. Like basketball, the point guard can only focus on being the best point guard he can be. It is not possible to commit yourself sincerely to be the best point guard if you too committed to making sure that your shooting guard is being the best shooting guard she can be. You can push her away or even cause her to make an error. Shooting guards, commit yourself to be the best shooting guard you can possibly be and allow your point guard to lead. Have faith in Coach G. Trust me, if that point guard isn't playing his position properly, he will not be leading your team much longer.

What I mean by that is be the best man or woman you can be. Play and focus on your position and the things you can control. You can only control your actions. You cannot control the actions of your teammates. Ladies, focus on playing your position the best you can. You cannot control him. No matter how much you search through his phone and try to make sure he is playing his position the right way, you are only distracting yourself from being the best at your position. You cannot do both; you are just going to have to have little trust and a hint of faith. If you cannot do that, you need to move on and get yourself another point guard.

Look at it this way, in the game of basketball, all the parties should have the same goal in mind, which is to win. The coach draws up the play, and the players head to play the game. The point guard communicates the play and then focuses on his position's obligations to make sure he does his part. There is a pass in basketball known as a no-look pass, which means the point guard is able to pass the ball without looking while believing that the shooting guard is playing his position properly. If she is, she will be in the exact position needed to receive that pass. The shooting guard has to trust that the point guard put the pass exactly where it needed to be caught and scoring should be easy. The coach can then sit on the bench with faith the that both players fully committed to their respected positions, and winning should be easy.

Sex Can Be Better

Is it fair to say that dating is different than it was in the past? We can agree that it is complicated, but why? If I had to narrow it down, I would have to say majority of the complication is contributed by sex. When did sex become a part of the dating package? In the past, sex was a wonderful addition to be included much later. In the generation in which I was raised, waiting to have sex was the expectation. The young ladies of that time were more fearful of the idea of sexual intercourse. The young men had no choice but to be patient. The act of engaging in oral sexual activities was like an unwritten law, which stated both parties agree that this is to be kept a secret. The repercussions following these acts at that time had the opportunity to be a young lady's nightmare such as public humiliation and the harsh judgement of her peers. The consequences outweigh the reward. That was more than enough motivation to refrain from having sex altogether. It was difficult being a curious young man growing up under the impression that all woman wanted to wait until marriage to have sex, so we had a challenge ahead of us if we wanted to detour that goal.

Things are completely different now. The young adults are not afraid of anything, let alone sex. This generation has turned sex into more of a hobby like it just something to do on a rainy day. Today, women are just as forthcoming when it comes to sex as the men. As a man, the anticipation of a sexual encounter with a woman has changed from wondering if it is going to happen to a matter of deciding when it will occur. This change in sexual activity causes the change in the style of dating. The idea of chivalry has not died. It has been substituted with the "I can buy you this and that" method. A lot of women have decided to accept this method and take full advantage of it but wonder why his pursuit is only sexual. What incentive are you giving a man to be a gentleman when he knows he can just go in his pocket and get just about anything he desires from you? When it comes to dating a woman and having sex these days, men have this sense of entitlement. When the opportunity presents itself, his expectation is to engage in some type of sexual encounter.

The unfortunate problem is we can fault women for this terrible perception that men have because a lot of woman have somehow adopted this unwritten rule of dating that states the moment a woman agrees to date a guy, she has also agreed to give him sex. He is your boyfriend, and you like him. I get it, but since when did that obligate you to sleep with him? Ladies, do you realize that it is this behavior that sends a man the wrong message that clouds his judgement therefore making his pursuit of you extremely sexual. The definition of courtship is a period during which a couple develops a romantic relationship especially with a view to marry. Ladies, can you imagine all the time, pain, and heartache you could have dodged if you had the ability to make a man with ill intentions give up and move on? Well, by deciding not to have casual sex with a man, you are empowered to dictate how that man will pursue you. This gives you a safety blanket that protects you from any man with the wrong intentions. This decision will assist you in filtering out any man who only want to pursue you sexually. His pursuit will be temporary because he has no intentions of being sexually patient with you.

The second definition of courtship is a behavior to persuade someone to marry, which means a man with the intentions to court you properly will chose to take a romantic route that will lead you to the altar and not the sexual route that only leads to the bedroom.

The question that arises now is, "Should a man and a woman truly wait until the marriage to have sex?" The answer is yes! However, my views on the marriage are different than most people. I feel that one of the key reasons marriages fail is because couples place too much emphasis on the ceremony and not enough time spent acknowledging the process of marriage, which is going before God. The act of going before God is the most important aspect of a marriage. The problem is when we think about getting married, we think about the wedding day. The date you set for your ceremony should not be the day you get married. If it is, it may be too late. The couple should already be married, and that ceremony should be the celebration of what they already have done before God.

Obtaining God's blessing should be done long before the couple decide on a wedding day. Honor God and get Him to cover your marriage by acknowledging that going before man and signing a few papers will not marry you, and the ceremony is just a celebration that allows the world to acknowledge your marriage. If the ceremony doesn't marry you, what does? Marriage should be a spiritual covenant between the two of you and God. The biggest misconception is that this happens on the wedding day. Contrary to that belief, this should be obtained long before then. The ceremony is the celebration of the couple legalizing their union for the world.

To obtain this covenant, ladies, you must require a man to find God before he finds you. You both must understand that God cannot be fooled for he knows your heart and cares not what your mouth says. Ladies, the dating process must be different, which means the removal of sex from the equation. Value yourself and your needs over the needs of any man and take time alone with God to prepare yourself as a wife. It is important to acknowledge that a man hasn't done anything for you until he make you his wife. Refusing to do wifey things for a boyfriend is the first step. This will cause a lot of guys to lose interest, which is great because they only wanted one thing. There will be a gentleman who will be intrigued with your decision to respect and value yourself, and he will support this decision. You see without sex you can truly get to know a person and build a foundation worth having, and if God is the head of this foundation, the path chosen shall surely lead to marriage.

Here is the missing link that is set to cover you long before the wedding day. The Bible tells us that when two or more people are gathered together in God's name, then we can expect Him to be there with them. This tells me that if a man and woman step in their closet at home face to face and go before God together, then He will be standing in the closet with them. What does that remind you of? The ceremony during which the pastor is symbolically standing in the place of God giving his blessing and pronouncing the couple husband and wife represents that gathering of two people. I believe if a couple truly loves each other unconditionally the way we all were intended to love and with a pure heart, they can then stand before God together and receive His spiritual covenant and be married in the eyes of the Lord.

We all can agree that sex to soon can be detrimental to the building of a relationship. The Bible tells us no sex before marriage. How many of us are doing that? Is that even possible? The way we view marriage today makes it seem impossible. A lot of couples date for 8 or 9 years before even considering marriage. God, you created sex, are you telling me to wait 9 years to enjoy the pleasures of sex? I honestly do not believe that He requires us to wait that long to enjoy the most pleasurable act on earth. Look at it this way; God does not sign off on any marriage certificates nor does He charge you for any of the wedding festivities. The wedding ceremony is for man. God asked that you come to Him and stated that a man who finds a wife will be blessed by the Lord because he has found a good thing. How can he receive that favor if he doesn't go before God with the wife he found? Ladies, waiting until marriage to have sex is simply holding out long enough for you and him to receive that spiritual covenant from God that marries you in His eyes.

The wedding day is not to be devalued by any means because all women deserve to have the wedding of their dreams, if desired. However, I want to reiterate to you that God does not sign off on any marriage certificate nor does He charge for any of the wedding festivities. What are you paying for? You paying for the celebration and the public acknowledgment of your marriage. I truly believe we would see an increase in the success rate of marriages, if more couples desired to go before God and receive His spiritual covenant before meeting at the altar. As a believer in God's word, I have faith that He is truly in the midst of the couple. If He approves of the union before Him, He will speak to them and send them both a heavy sense of conviction that will fill their hearts with certainty. That certainty provides an answer to the question, "How do you know the person before you is the one?" Well, I would then argue that God told me, and I am sure I can trust His accuracy.

Now, when a couple is married under the spiritual covenant, can the couple then have sex? Absolutely! You are now married in the eyes of the Lord, and that is really all that matters. Conviction is the work of the Holy Spirit during which people are able to see themselves as God sees them, so I think we should change the standard from waiting till marriage to waiting until we can honestly say we feel truly convicted by God. This can only be obtained by the true undeniable movement of God's hand on your heart and His voice in your ear. Look at it this way; How can waiting to get married really be enough when hypothetically, any two people can meet and decide to get married? Does that truly get it right with God and give them the clearance to have sex? I believe the objective behind waiting till marriage was to wait long enough to receive God's covenant and to bring to better sex the way God intended.

Sex is a beautiful thing and is the reason we are all alive today. The generations to come depend on it. God created sex for us all to enjoy; however, I believe aspect of waiting to have sex was implemented by God as a way of challenging us mentally. We serve a God who understands the powers of our flesh and how difficult it is to restrain them. The object is for sex to be better. Giving us a choice to wait to enjoy sex is a test of our obedience. As I stated earlier in the text, my understanding of waiting to get married means waiting on God and receiving His spiritual covenant first. How long it takes God to convict us is the true challenge. Are you strong enough to hold out long enough for God to bless your union? This dilemma reminds me of a choice given to Adam once he was placed in the Garden of Eden.

Allow me to give you an alternative view on why I believe that waiting on God is the key to better sex. Adam was placed in the Garden of Eden and was forbidden from consuming the fruit of the Tree of Life and the Tree of Knowledge of Good and Evil. They were faced with a choice to be obedient or go against God. Well, men, we are faced with the same decision. A woman's body symbolizes the Tree of Life because she can give life. My take on God's command is that Adam was not ready for the knowledge he would obtain from eating the fruit. His lack of obedience and patience as he consumed the fruit too soon made everything change. That could be a direct correlation on why things tend to change when a couple has sex too soon. Prior to the couple having sex, the man has no knowledge of what it tastes nor feels like to have sex with the woman. My guess is with the choice to be obedient and wait on God, He would have made the fruit sweeter and more enjoyable for Adam once he was mentally and physically ready to receive such knowledge. How can sex be better? Sex can be better with the choice to be obedient and wait to obtain God's spiritual covenant before having sex.

All men should be mentally and physically ready before taking a woman's body because sex can draw couple closer together or tear them apart. The only thing that truly makes sex different is how you feel about a person mentally, so in exercising restraint and giving yourself time to wait to receive God's covenant, you are able to prepare yourself to receive your partner. This wait allows the couple to work on themselves and bring on the mental, physical and spiritual growth needed to be married. The man and woman are also able to build the foundation and the mental connection needed for them to respect and enjoy better sex the way He intended.

Temptation is the work of the devil. He wants us to go against God, and he understands the powers of the flesh, so he speaks to it. However, God works through faith and wants us to operate in it by choosing to sacrifice the flesh to obey Him. The idea of waiting for marriage is to wait on God's confirmation that the couple is equally yoked, compatible, and mentally ready to enjoy marriage the way He intended it to be. Then and only then will the couple be strong enough to handle the knowledge of sex and commit to each other unconditionally and resist the temptations of infidelity.

Her Hurt Is All His Fault

Guilt can kill you, literally. In 2015, a friend of mine tried to kill himself out of guilt that all the pain the mother of his child endured was his fault. This was hard for family and friends to understand because the two of them had never been together as a couple. Marcus and Kim went to college together. Kim was the quiet type with very few friends. She took school very serious. Marcus, however, was a football player and very popular with the ladies. Marcus noticed Kim in the café at the school and had no idea who she was, so he approached her and introduced himself. Kim knew exactly who Marcus was, and she was not impressed to say the least, so she politely spoke and continued to her seat. Marcus stood there with a look of disappointed confusion and decided to let Kim be to save himself the embarrassment of rejection in front of his peers.

Kim and a few classmates decided to attend the football game that following Friday. Kim became a fan of Marcus the night of the game. Watching him excel in his element made Kim look at Marcus in a different light. Marcus played well that night, and as he exited the field, he made sure to give Kim a wave. To his surprise, she smiled and waved back. Marcus approached Kim on the school yard the next day and said, "I was happy to see you at the game last night." Kim, more receptive this time, replied, "I am surprised you even noticed me over all the other girls!" They began conversing, and to Kim's surprise, she actually enjoyed the conversation and wanted more of it.

As they began hanging out around school more and more, Kim started to develop feelings for Marcus, and he seemed to have mutual feelings for her, but Kim couldn't understand why he hadn't asked her out. Kim's friends told her it was because Marcus only wanted one thing, and she should just leave him alone. Kim believed her friends to be jealous. She decided to let Marcus how she was feeling, and he ensured her that he also had feelings for her, but he was not ready for a relationship. Marcus then invited her to a party later that night off campus. Reluctantly, Kim accepted. Kim figured one way to get Marcus to like her more was to loosen up a bit, so she decided to let her hair down and have a little fun that night.

Kim arrived at the party, and the first thing she saw was Marcus in what appeared to be a very intimate conversation with a young lady. Instead of leaving, she decided to get herself a drink and hold true to the thought of loosening up and having fun. Marcus noticed Kim approximately one hour and 3 drinks later dancing closely with a random guy at the party. He decided to intervene. Kim, unhappy with Marcus, pushed him away as she made her way back to the table to get another drink. Marcus decided to have a drink of his own. Eventually, the two started to dance and drink together. It was getting extremely late, and the party was coming to an end. Kim was clearly intoxicated and told Marcus that she could not drive. Marcus had no intentions of taking Kim to her house and decided to take her to his place where they shared kisses for the first time. One thing led to another, and the next morning Kim woke up next to Marcus with her clothes next to the television. Kim sat there looking back at Marcus with a slight smile on her face. She was happy initially, but that feeling was short lived and replaced with regret as Marcus awoke and went directly into the bathroom without a word.

Kim was lost with thoughts racing through her head and watched as Marcus came out of the bathroom fully clothed. His first words to her were, "Don't you have class today?" with her clothes in hand. Absolutely stunned, all Kim could do was take her clothes and put them on. The ride to back to campus was quiet and seemed so long. Luckily for Kim, when she reached her apartment, her roommate had already left for class, and she was able to shower. Kim could have filled the tub up with tears as she tried desperately to scrub away his scent and his touch, but no soap in the world could wash away the thought of last night. Avoiding Marcus at all cost was not going to be easy and became impossible weeks later when Kim woke up with morning sickness. She found out that she was 6 weeks pregnant, and an abortion was not an option but neither was telling Marcus. Kim decided to discontinue her education and move back home.

Just over 3 years later, Marcus got a promotion that required him to relocate to Atlanta, GA. After being in the city for less than a month, he ran into a very familiar face in the grocery store. Marcus ran up to her with excitement. Kim never expected to see him again and thought she saw a ghost. Marcus insisted that she allow him to buy her lunch. Kim declined nicely as she bent to pick up her daughter. Marcus congratulated and complemented Kim on her beautiful little girl as he handed her his business card. He asked that she please allow him that lunch, and Kim walked off. Marcus watched days pass and he wished to get a call from Kim. He got his wish about a week later when Kim called, and they agreed to meet up for lunch. Marcus arrived at the restaurant before Kim purposely, so he could stand there with a rose in hand and watch her walk in. He quickly noticed that something was not right. Kim walked over, and as soon as the two embraced, she began to cry. Marcus sat her down and asked her to drink some water to calm down and tell him what happened.

Kim explained how sorry she was. Marcus was so confused because he insisted they have lunch together to give him the opportunity to apologize for his actions in college. He explained how young and immature he was. Kim stopped him and just asked him to listen. She went on and explained that for the last 2 years, she was in a relationship with a very bad man who was very controlling, and he hit her. She feared not only for her life but the life of her daughter. Marcus attempted to console her and told her everything will be OK. Kim begun to cry profusely as she struggled to say that she recently found out that the guy she is with had been molesting her daughter. Marcus didn't know what to say, and with Kim's next statement, his whole world was crushed. Kim mumbled, "Marcus, she is your daughter."

Marcus paused, gathered his thoughts and asked firmly, "What did you say?" Kim continued to cry as she told him repeatedly that she was his daughter until Marcus embraced her. All he could do was hold her with endless thoughts going through his head. Marcus full of mixed emotions found himself battling with his spirit. He wanted to be angry, and he had every right to be furious, right? How could she not tell him? How could she be so selfish? These questions flew through his mind because for some strange reason, he understood. Kim expected Marcus to be angry. Marcus started praying and asking for forgiveness. Kim was so confused. Marcus then grabbed the steak knife and cut his wrist! Kim started screaming, and Marcus in a blank stare began to bleed more and more.

Marcus was rushed to the hospital, and they made it just in time. He lost a lot of blood, but the good news was he did not cut the major artery in his wrist and would be OK. Laying in the hospital for the next few days on suicide watch, Marcus was able to spend some alone time with God. Well, he was not truly alone time because Kim never left his side, and every night when family and friends left, the two would just pray together. God was able to heal them both and bring spiritual, mental, and physical growth to their lives in that short period of time.

On was the last day Marcus was scheduled to be in the hospital, Kim's mother brought her some bad but good news. The man who she was dating has been arrested after running through a stop sign. Apparently, he did not have a current driver's license or a prescription for the pills and the boat load of marijuana he had in his possession. Moreover, he was not aware of the warrant out for his arrest for violating the terms of his probation. He was going to jail and would not be bother Kim anytime soon. This news brought tears of joy to Kim's eyes. Her mother hugged her and told her, "See how easy it is when you let God fight your battles."

It was at this time when Marcus helped shaped the alternative view for this chapter. He got up and walked over to Kim and took her by the hand. He looked her in her eyes and said that he was sorry and asked that she forgive him for being selfish by cutting his wrist. He stated that his daughter hasn't had her father all this time, and his actions would have ensured that she never would. He told her that he was angry when she told him what she was going though, and that Mia was his daughter but made it clear that he was not angry at her at all. He was angry at himself. Marcus said that every moment of her pain was his fault! Kim said, "How can you say that?" Marcus continued to say, "Yes, all your pain is my fault, and I take full responsibility. It started with me as a man back in college. I pursued you in the wrong way from the beginning. I was a young guy not thinking about the pain my actions could cause and the scars I could leave. I was only thinking about one thing, and for that I am sorry!"

He continued, "Kim, your world was completely different before I came in it with ill intentions. I am the reason you decided to leave school, and I get why you didn't tell me you were pregnant, and I can't say I blame you. Kim, you understood I was not fit to be a father, and for that I thank you! By not telling me, you protected me from myself by not allowing me to reject my daughter. I am the reason you are a single mother, and I am the reason you were broken. Now, there is no way I can get that time back nor repay you for laying on that table and having my child alone, but I am willing to spend the rest of my life trying." He got one knee and asked, "Will You Marry Me?" Kim said, "I can't answer that right now, but you can start by trying to convince her!" As Marcus turned around, Kim's mother was walking little Mia into the room. Marcus broke down in tears as he hugged Mia for the first time.

As a man, I can honestly say that when we gain interest in a woman, we do not think about it this way, but we should. I should consider my true intentions before I go drag myself into the world of that beautiful woman with so much promise and purpose. I understand that as a man I can have a huge impact on her, and that can influence her future. Do I want to make her life harder? Do I want to be the reason she feels pain? Do I want to talk to her negatively and lower her self-esteem? Do I want to make her a single mom who ends up with a man who is not good to her or my child? Do I want to be that guy? If I can't confidently answer those questions with a firm "No!," I should just leave that woman alone. As I man of God, I understand His promise. There is a woman out here who I will meet, and I will desire nothing more than to treat her better than she has ever been treated. She may even come with scars of her own, insecurities, and a broken heart, but I can't wait to help her pick up the pieces, forget she has ever been hurt, and ensure she will never feel that way again! Yes, let me take my time and find her.

In case you were wondering, Marcus and Kim have been married for over 2 years now. Kim is working on her master's degree, and little Mia is a spoiled daddy's girl.

Just Ask Her to Marry You

Marriage is supposed to be the goal, right? Have you ever sat back and asked yourself, "What's the point of the casual dating phase? Why don't we just skip it?" A lot earlier in life, no one dated for months or even years, so when did it start and why? What is accomplished during the time we are casually dating? We all know of a couple who has been dating for years. They may even consider themselves technically married. This couple lives together, and they have kids together, so it's safe to say that they have the dynamics of a married couple. However, forget the technicality, this couple is not married, and it may be nowhere in sight. Couples like this understand the dynamics of their relationship and seem to be content with the way things are and see no point in rushing into a marriage even though it has been several years.

Now, there are some couples who do not desire to get married, and I respect and understand that; however, these are not the couples I am referencing. There are people in these types of relationships who would love and even wish to be married. I have 2 friends. One is male and the other female; my male friend has been in his relationship for 3 years. He would love to get married someday. He just would like to be sure of a few things first before he decides to propose. He would like to ensure that he can afford to be in a marriage even though it is unclear what that means. It's up for interpretation. He would like to buy her the ring she desires, afford the ceremony and reception, and pay for all the food with no problem. It makes perfect sense, right? Well, I just so happen to know his lovely lady personally as well, and she has confirmed verbally on multiple occasions that she loves him and would be more than happy to wait on the ring and marry him in the backyard with finger foods if that will make her his wife. She is constantly joking about leaving him if he does not propose soon.

Being the good friend that I am to him, I challenged him to remind me of his reasoning for continuing to date with no form of progression with this woman who has confessed her love for him and her desire to be his wife. I told him, "You love her, and you've said that you have no doubt that this woman is going to be your wife, so why haven't you at least made the next step and propose to her?" He was honest with me and told me his hesitations come from the mistakes he has made in the past. He is not sure he is ready. He has cheated continuously for the last 2 years, and he is afraid that he may have serious feelings for someone else. He plans to iron all of that out before he takes that step to be 100% focused and committed. I respect that; however, I do not understand it because you can do all of that as a single man and not get into a relationship until you feel you are ready to be 100% focused and committed.

My female friend's situation is a little different than my male friend. She is currently single due to the casual dating phase, she felt that the two of them should have dated casually much longer before he considered proposing to her. The couple had a wonderful relationship. They were childhood friends who grew up together, so they were very familiar with each other. They may have dated for 4 months before he decided to propose. I was just as shocked as he was when her response to his proposal was, "Not right now!" It brought a change to their relationship. Shortly after that, she decided to end it. Being the good friend that I am, I made it clear to her that I did not understand her decision. He is good to her and treats her like a queen, and she loves that about him. She trusts him wholeheartedly, and he is God-fearing and an example of what a man of God should be. What was the problem? Her reasoning was it felt right, but it was just too soon in spite of the fact that she has known him her entire life.

These two scenarios created a question for me, and I have been trying to figure it out. I know of couples who have dated for years and never got engaged as well as couples who have been engaged for years, and the result was not marriage. My question is, "What's the difference between being in a relationship and being engaged? A fiance' and a girlfriend? Neither guarantees anything, and there is no written law that dictates or limits the time frame a couple can be engaged, so why not instead of asking her to be his girlfriend ask her to be his fiancé? There are too many of us who do not take relationships seriously in the dating phase. We mess around, lie, and cheat, and like my male friend, we feel that the moment we get engaged we will correct this behavior. We never do even after being engaged. So, I wonder is that the difference? When we are dating, are we not serious about the person, and once we get engaged are we serious now? When we should have been serious from day one!!

No women truly sign up to be played with for years. If that was the case, she would have never entered the relationship. In so many words, the way we operate now is exactly what we are signing her up for until we get engaged. It's to my understanding that as a woman, the idea of meeting a man that initially wants to make your his Fiance', sounds absolutely crazy. However, if you had your choice between two relationship paths, which would you chose? The path where the man was honest enough to tell you his plan is to make you his girlfriend, and during this time, he plans to lie and mess around on you until he decide to propose, and then he promises to correct his behavior and treat you the way you deserve to be treated? Or would you choose the path where the man desires to make you his fiance', and during this time, he plans to treat you like the queen you are and continue this for as long as it takes for him to make you his wife?

When dating, so many people say that marriage should be the goal. If this is truly the case, why would it be crazy for a man to ask a woman for her hand in marriage from the beginning and skip the dating phase? Theoretically, there is no difference between the two phases, or it shouldn't be. It is very possible for a man to meet a woman of interest and ask her to marry him with the understanding that this is not to take place any time soon. The couple can be engaged for as long as they like and take their sweet time getting to know each other. These are typically all the things we normally do when we date. The only difference is he has been committed from day one. Again, if marriage is truly the goal, then in doing it this way, the couple is in the engagement phase working towards the goal of marriage versus being in the dating phase and working towards the engagement. Getting engaged does not obligate you to anything, so like the dating phase, if the engagement fails for any reason, the couple then can decide to exit the relationship.

Ladies, the alternative view is to require him pursue you properly from day one as he would if you were his "fiancé." You are meant to be courted, and that starts the moment he wants something more than a friendship from you. To court is to be involved with someone romantically with the intention of marrying. If that is not the goal in the dating phase, then what purpose does it serve? The answer cannot be to get to know each other because that's an ongoing process that will take place in any phase and continue even after you marry. The truth of the matter is dating with no purpose is pointless, and dating with the intentions to marry is called courting, which takes place in the engagement phase. The idea is to make her your fiancé and not your girlfriend. This way your intentions and motives are known so that the progression is towards the goal and not towards courting properly.

She Must Have Made Him Herself

When I went off to college, it was my first time away from home, and I was a little homesick. I remember my mother telling me to find a good church home, and people there will be my family away from home. That is exactly what happen, I attended First Baptist Church of Warner Robins, GA. There, I met a motherly figure by the name of Kimberly Barnes, and she became adopted mother so to say. Mrs. Barnes was amazing. She was so educated and well put together. I secretly had a major crush on Mrs. Barnes. She was much older, but she was gorgeous. I would always joke about, "If my future wife doesn't age like her once we are older, I am leaving". Mrs. Barnes helped me in so many ways. She tried her best to mold me and counsel me on how to formulate a good relationship with a woman. The biggest lesson came from Mrs. Barnes indirectly by the way she praised her husband. Initially, I was blind and unreceptive to the message. Granted, I was 20 at the time and had no knowledge of what the scripture says about how a man should love his wife to make her speak of him this way. I just figured all wives praised and spoke highly of their husbands in that manner, so her words fell on deaf ears.

All of that changed the day I headed to take my vehicle into the shop for service repairs, and it decided to shut down on me. I was stranded. I called Mrs. Barnes, and she said she was on the way. When she arrived, her husband whom I never had the pleasure of meeting was with her. I greeted him and told him I felt like I knew him because Mrs. Barnes spoke so highly of him, and his response was "Likewise". The couple was on their way to the mall when I called. I was in the process of dropping my car off for service which was going to take a while, so they invited me to tag alone with them. As I was riding alone in the back seat, I immediately started to take notice of Mr. and Mrs. Barnes behavior. They had been married for 13 years, so why was he still driving and holding her hand? Why was she talking and smiling at him like they had been away from each other for a year or something like that? It seemed a bit much to me.

Once we arrived at the mall and parked, Mr. Barnes got out of the vehicle. Mrs. Barnes did not move a muscle nor did she reach for the door handle, so I closed my door back. I thought the two us were staying in the car. Mr. Barnes came around and opened her door and assisted her in getting out of the car. I was thinking to myself, "He can stop it now. There is no way he can consciously keep up this façade". As we were walking, Mr. Barnes and I conversed about sports, and as we reached the entrance of the mall, Mrs. Barnes literally stopped in her tracks to allow Mr. Barnes to open the door for her. Oh, how I wanted to ask her, "If he had not opened the door, would you still be standing there?" I felt every bit in my spirit the answer would have been "Yes!"

As I followed closely behind as they shopped, I noticed how Mr. Barnes would just do things most men would have to be asked to do. It just seemed as if he was always one step ahead. I cannot recall one time she had to ask him to hold something because he already had it.

We decided to grab a bite to eat from the food court, and I noticed Mrs. Barnes wasn't concerned with the food at all. She simply communicated that she would find us a table. Now, one of the biggest struggles for a man is getting a straight answer from a woman when he asks her, "What do you want to eat?" The answer 99% of the time is "I don't know". Imagine my surprise when Mr. Barnes was able to avoid that question and bring her food without having to get up again. He knew exactly what she wanted and how she wanted it.

I spoke to Mrs. Barnes a few days later about my thoughts, and she open my eyes and helped me see things completely differently. She stated that her peers have similar perspectives. They believe she may have made him herself and rightfully so. Mrs. Barnes explained that she and Mr. Barnes only courted for a short period, and in this time, he was able to show her that he was the perfect man for her, and the feeling was mutual because he wasted no time asking her to marry him. This struck my curiosity. I clearly understood how he could feel that she was the perfect woman for him, but how did he give her the confidence that he was the perfect man for her? Mrs. Barnes's next statement formulated the alternative view for this chapter when she said, "It was more her fault than his, and he was just forced to be himself".

I then asked her to elaborate, and she followed that by asking me to spell the word "together." After I was able to spell the word successfully, we scrambled up a pen and paper, and she then asked me to write out the word. After I completed the writing of the word, she requested that I give her the paper, so I did. She said, "Now, as a man, once you get together with a woman, how do you suppose you can stay together?" I gave her the best generic answer I could think of. She smiled and then handed me the paper back that I wrote the word "together" on. She took the liberty of making a small modification to the word that would answer the question she previously asked. The modification looked like this "to/get/her." She said a man has a higher chance at a successful relationship with a woman if he continues doing the things he did to get her in the first place.

At the time, this was mind blowing information for me. If I want to stay together, do not stop doing what I did to get her. This made total sense, but I reminded her that this still does not tell me what Mr. Barnes did to show you he was the perfect man for you. She reiterated that the credit was hers and not Mr. Barnes because of the decision she made for herself that dictated the actions of Mr. Barnes and made it easy him to continue to do the things he did in the beginning to get her. The decision she made for herself was to remain a mystery to Mr. Barnes to ensure his actions were personality traits. She said the common mistake that women make when dating a man is to give too many details. Typically, when a man a woman meet, they desire to get to know each other. The first date is like one of a job interview that consists of a series of questions. These questions can range anywhere from "What are you looking for?" to "Can you tell me all about you?" The man may ask questions concerning the woman's personality, her past relationships, and all the mistakes the last gentlemen did to lose his place in her life. Mrs. Barnes made the decision that she was not going to answer any of those question, and she made that very clear to him. Initially, Mr. Barnes was not receptive to this decision. He had trouble understanding how it would be possible for two people to get to know each other without discussing their past.

At that moment, Mrs. Barnes said that she had a decision to make. She could choose him and decide to change her way of thinking to make him more comfortable, or she could choose herself and stand firm in her decision even if that meant leaving him in an uncomfortable state. She chose herself, and to her surprise, Mr. Barnes said he did not understand, but he respected her decision and was willing to give it a try. Mrs. Barnes said this was intriguing to her, and he gained some serious points with her. A man who was willing to be uncomfortable for her was already off to a good start. Mrs. Barnes helped me to understand her way of thinking by giving me the reason behind the decision. She said the typical way of dating is to answer all those questions and tell the gentleman all of things the last man did wrong, the things she liked versus the things she did not agree with, and all the things she wished had been different.

She felt that by women doing it the typical way, they were setting themselves up for failure. This is the reason why it's common for a woman to be manipulated by the representative of a man in the beginning. This is a man who portrays himself to be one way in the beginning to gain a woman's trust and attention only to let her down months later once the real version of him surfaces. Mrs. Barnes said women do not deserve to be misled in this manner; however, they are at fault for giving the man all the answers to the test. When a woman answers all the questions, essentially what she is doing is telling him how to treat her, and subconsciously, his behavior will reflect the things he was told because of his initial interest level in the woman. This is short lived because of the effort it takes to keep up the façade.

Mrs. Barnes decided she would remain a mystery to a man to help him exhibit his personality traits other than behaving in the way he was told. She believed time reveals all, and she preferred Mr. Barnes to learn how to treat her rather than tell him. She asked me if I questioned my current employer in my interviewer. She wanted to know if asked them, "How was the last man that held this position?" and "What are some of the things he did wrong?" so I know not to do them. I laughed and said, "No, I definitely didn't ask those questions." Mrs. Barnes told me this was because I was not concerned with the last man to hold the position, and she was right; honestly, I could care less about the last man who held the position. I was focused and determined to obtain the position for myself despite the rationale for parting ways with the last man. My goal was to ensure them that if they selected me, I would work the position to the best of my ability.

Well, this was the goal behind Mrs. Barnes's decision the moment she decided she was tired of being surprised at the drastic change in a man's behavior months down the road. I asked her, "How did Mr. Barnes show her he was the perfect man for you?" Well, it was Mrs. Barnes showing herself all women have several things that they love and desire in a man, and more importantly, all women have different love languages that speak directly to the heart. The question that Mrs. Barnes posed was, "Why would I tell him those things and allow him to pretend that these behaviors are a part of his personality." By not doing so, Mrs. Barnes quickly was able to filter out the men who were unable to speak to her heart. Mrs. Barnes s said one of the major things that spoke to her heart was for a man to open the car door for her. On the first date, if she told a man this was the key to her heart, regardless if he like doing it or not, moving forward, you can be sure that he will be opening the door to the car for her every chance he got. At that point, how would she determine if this kind gesture was a part of who he was or simply the knowledge that this was a sure way to her heart?

Now, imagine she kept that desire to herself and went out with a man and not once did he attempt to open her car door. That's a clear indication that this man may not be the man for her. It's beginning signs like this that a woman should not ignore for the simple fact that it is impossible for a woman to keep all these major desires to herself and go out with a man, and he exhibits all those characteristics that she desires. This is a clear indication that his actions are part of his character, and for the most part, she can be confident that he will not change months down the road because typically personality traits do not change.

In Mrs. Barnes's situation, she encouraged Mr. Barnes to work the position to the best of his ability by focusing on the woman she is now and the woman she is becoming and not to attempt to formulate how he will operate based on who she was and past situations. He graciously accepted, and they began dating. He made small mistakes, but he was man enough to acknowledge them and by learning from them, he was able quickly to adjust his actions. Mrs. Barnes said she was just blown away with all the things that she desired for Mr. Barnes to do and before she knew it, he would do them, or they were already done, which caused everyone to think she must have made him herself

I Am So in Like with You

Ionce sent someone a message, and it read, "I am so in like with you." She replied, "Did you mean love?," and this opened a dialog on love. I said exactly what I meant, but she did not receive it because she did not understand the meaning, and she even rejected it. The word "like" was not good enough. It didn't paint a clear enough picture for this person to describe how I felt at the time. Why was that the case? What is love? Love is a lot of things. Love is kind, joyous, and patient. We all want to find love and anticipate falling in love as we should; love is a beautiful thing. However, love can also be painful because losing love can hurt like a knife in the chest. Love can also be confusing and misinterpreted. Love can even be dangerous because love can be lust defined as a strong sexual desire that makes people behave inappropriately or even aggressively.

Love is defined as an intense feeling of deep attraction; however, it is debatable because love is a feeling or emotion. If I am one to believe that love is an emotion, then like all emotions, love can be controlled. This leaves me to believe that love is a choice; it is simply a decision that can be accepted or rejected. That may explain why falling in love is easy to do. Falling in love is almost effortless, but losing that loving feeling is also very easy to do.

The decisions some of us make out of love or for love is not always of God; however, I do believe that God is love. This is one of the main supporting factors that leads me to believe that love is a choice. God loves us all and went through great heights to display that love for us, but He allows us the power to act without constraints and the ability to act at our own discretion which is what we all know as the power of free will. Free will is ultimately a choice given even when it comes to obeying, serving, and even loving God.

"Love" appears 310 times in 280 verses in the King James Version of the Bible, so it's safe to say that God is love. If God allows us the choice to love Him or not, I don't think it would be far fetched to say we have the choice to love each other. However, though we can choose to love or not, we all are still brothers and sisters in Christ, so it is instilled in us to love each other. Don't you think it is in us to love? We don't wish death on our worst enemy. You may say what you may; however, if the person you disliked the most died in front of you, you would feel a level of remorse. That is a form of love that comes from God telling us to love our neighbor the way we love ourselves.

"Like," on the other hand, is different. The word is defined as *having the same characteristics or qualities* or as a verb it means *to find agreeable or even enjoyable*. These definitions clearly tell me the choice to like someone is not mine; either I will like someone, or I will not. "Like" and "love" are both extremely important; however, I am finding that "like" tends to have a slight edge on "love." As a child, you are taught to love, and as you grow up, you learned to like or dislike. No matter your decision, if something or someone is not agreeable to you, you will find it difficult to like them; however, you may choose to love them. We all have met individuals, and for some odd reason or another, with or without facts, we may like or dislike them. I am sure that we all have individuals in our life who we do not like, but we love them anyhow.

The Alternative view in this chapter allows you to look at it this way. In a relationship, it is more important to be in like more so than in love. I much rather someone like me a lot than love me. I say this because again it is in us to love each other, which means love is a choice, and love can be controlled. That also tells me love can take care of itself. People cannot choose to like me. Either they will like me, or they will not. The body follows the mind, so if you tell yourself you love someone consistently enough, eventually, you will start to believe that. What you believe alters your behavior therefore making it a reality for yourself. However, if you tell yourself you like someone, and you do not, you will not. You may try as hard as you like. If that person does not possess similar characteristics or qualities, liking them will be difficult. The number one way of expressing your love for someone is to simply tell them, "I love you," and that is acceptable and meaningful. How is it possible that we can believe and even defend that someone loves us without him or her showing it though his or her actions? Is it because that's what we chose to believe because he or she told us so? However, when it comes to liking someone, our expectations are completely different. Just telling someone you like him or her is not enough. You must show that person through your actions, or he or she will believe that you do not mean what you say. Have you ever been in a situation in which thought to yourself based off this person's actions there is no possible way this person can like me? I have experienced this feeling once or twice in my life.

One of the beginning stages of a relationship is called the honeymoon phase. This is the stage that everyone enjoys the most, but let's call it what it is. It is the liking stage during which we are so in like with each other. We all would agree in the liking stage, things are wonderful. Our focus is on the other person and making him or her happy. Our communication is even different. A woman would agree that the man who told her he liked her in the beginning is not the man telling her he loves her now. Why is this the case? Isn't the liking stage the reason we all fall in love in the first place? Why is it our expectation that this phase will end for sure? Why do we believe that it is unrealistic to think that we can maintain the honeymoon phase forever? I believe that might just be one of the problems. It all starts with our beliefs that we bring to fruition.

In the beginning of a relationship when we are liking each other, we text and talk on the phone all the time. We make plans to see each other as much as possible. We just enjoy each other's company that much. Liking each other brings proverbial butter-flies to you both when you think of the other person, and you both are happy; the relationship seems to be so easy and free. Then, the inevitable happens. You choose to fall in love, and then the dynamics of the relationship tend to change. It seems we become so possessive and extremely serious. All the fun is drained from the relationship. All the reasons that brought the two together seem to have been forgotten, and all the negative actions, anger, and loveless arguments are excused by the perception that this is the way it is when two people are in love. The belief that a person treating you badly is out of love is ridiculous to me.

Look at it this way. It is not the fact that we are in love with our best friend; however, we do have a form of love for him or her, which again proves it is in us to love. However, this ability to love exists mostly because he or she possesses similar characteristics that are agreeable to us so much so that we like and enjoy him or her enough to love and respect the relationship we have with this person. This reality allows for a different more effective way of communicating. When you disagree with a best friend, you would hate to lose that relationship. You honor that the bond so much that you make a conscience effort to think about your delivery and communicate effectively to convey how you are feeling. You are receptive and listen to him or her and take his or her feelings into consideration. If things do get out of hand, pride is often put to the side to repair, save or not to jeopardize the relationship with your best friend. We trust our best friend with our life and defend him or her if necessary even if he or she is wrong. We like him or her that much.

When it comes to the person we love and are in a relationship with, why do we see red when we argue and fight like cats and dogs? We refuse to communicate with the person or feel with simply cannot. We may be wrong, but we are so prideful in our relationship that we refuse to say sorry. We don't completely trust the person we are with because we operate in so much fear of being hurt by him or her. We try to micromanage the relationship by searching for things that would be detrimental to the relationship. It is hard to believe that any of us agree to a relationship when the perception is everybody cheats, so we look for it every chance we get. Unfaithfulness is the expectation, so we go through phones and things of that nature. It is like we want to sabotage the relationship instead of enjoying it with faith that we can be happy not realizing these are the reasons we push the other person away.

What essentially happens is you fall out of like. It is possible to lose the loving feeling once you fall out of like, but it is not possible to stop loving. Remember, it is in us to love, so you will love always. How many people of your past do you dislike, but you admit you still love them? When you stop liking them, it made it impossible to feel love, which is the reason people cheat on the person they love with the person they like. This tells me that the secret to a successful relationship is to focus on continuing to like each other every day, and because God instilled love in us, it will take care of itself. Since it is easy to love and not like but nearly impossible to really like and not feel love, let's stay in like.

What Kind of Trophy Are You?

When I was 9 years old, I started playing youth basketball. I fell in love with the sport and became extremely competitive. I would fuel this competitive nature of mine before every game by asking myself, "Why do I play?" and responding, "To win!" I have always been told that in everything I do, give it my all, and I will be rewarded. Well, for a few seasons playing youth basketball, the reward was a certificate and a ribbon to congratulate us on a good season. Near the end of my first year playing AAU basketball, I was told that a trophy was in sight. I remember thinking to myself, "I have to win that trophy!" I became a different player as if being competitive was not enough. I became extremely motivated and obsessed with the idea of winning a trophy.

I went to the coach and told him that I was willing to do anything to win. I wanted to work harder than before and motivate my teammates to match my work ethic. I was so passionate in practice and laser-focused in the games. We had a good team, and with every win, I felt myself getting closer and closer to that trophy. Unfortunately, we lost 3 of the last 5 games making us ineligible to enter the championship tournament to compete for my trophy. A few short weeks later, my coach held an end-of-season banquet and gave individual accolades in the form of a small trophy. The entire team got a trophy even the team managers for their contribution during the season. Despite the rationale for the trophy that the coach gave, I looked at it as a participation trophy. I remember getting home that night and having to return to the car to retrieve the trophy to show my father. It broke shortly afterwards. I was not by any means proud of this trophy.

When the school year started, I had a few months before the basketball season started, but I needed a reason to stay after school, so I joined the chess club. My father was the only person I have ever played in the game of chess, so I figured it was just a fun way pass time. When I joined the club, it was just supposed to be something to do to keep from going home in the afternoon. I took a liking to it once it dawned on me that these kids took this seriously, and to my surprise, they talked a lot of trash. I quickly realized it was no different than a one-on-one game of basketball, and at that moment, my competitive nature took over. I sat down at the first available table to play my first game, and I came out victoriously. I felt pretty good about myself until the chess teacher walked in, and behind her were 5 students. One of them was carrying the biggest trophy I had ever seen. I immediately looked at the student I just defeated and asked him who these students were.

These 5 students were chess champions. They won the state competition the previous year. The young man holding the trophy decided he was going to display it in the classroom for the year as motivation. I then decided I wanted a trophy like that for myself. I wanted to challenge him just to see how I would match up against the elite players in the club. I was required to establish myself as one of the better players before I got my opportunity to face off with him. I got my chance 3 weeks later, and I must say he beat me rather quickly and was very arrogant about it. This kid was more than confident; he was rude. We had a small verbal debate until he proved his point by pointing to trophy and announcing to the class that I could never beat him, and the day I do, the trophy is mine. I went home angry that day. When I got home, I talked to my father about it, and he told me that nobody is going to just give something like that to me, and I would have to earn it.

I went to my room, and I cleaned off the bookshelf to make room for the trophy I planned to win and sit there. I dedicated myself to becoming a better player. I would play my father and lose, but this time I would focus on trying to understand why I lost and how to improve. I hated losing, but I had to humble myself completely. Despite losing game after game to every kid in the club, I gained knowledge about the game of chess after each loss. The day came that I felt I was ready to challenge him for the trophy. I walked into the classroom and sat directly in front of that young man with all the other kids gathered around us. The game was on. I rushed home that afternoon with trophy in hand, and to my surprise, my father had a trophy case waiting on me. I was so happy. I felt honored as I placed my beautiful trophy in its new place. Every morning, I would wake up and just stare at it. I may have used all my mother's glass cleaner on it trying to keep it shining!

One thing I believe all men have in common is a level of competitiveness. In some form or fashion, we all love to compete. We love to attack a challenge head on, and we all are very prideful, so when we really set our mind on winning, failing becomes impossible. We feed off the sense of accomplishment, so the greater the challenge, the bigger the reward. By no means do we want it easy. The harder that both men and women work for something we want, the more we value it. Ladies, understand that to win is why we play the game. No man in any sport wants to put in all his effort, blood, sweat, fight, and even tears and allow another man to walk away with the trophy. The trophy is a constant reminder of how hard he worked, so he will cherish it with his heart and be proud to show it off to the world.

Ladies, realizing that all men want a trophy, it is up to you to decide what type of trophy you are going to be. You can allow yourself to be a participation trophy, one that every man gets with little to no effort at all. This trophy has no sentimental value and is possessed with very little care. You may find this trophy broken and left behind, or you can decide that you are going to be that beautiful championship trophy, which only the best man wins. That trophy is something that man must prove himself worthy of possessing by humbling himself and learning how to put himself in the best position to win it. That trophy is something that he will clear room in his life for way before he wins it.

That trophy will make him feel honored after he wins it. He will cherish it, love it and show it off to the world. This is the trophy that he worked so hard for that he will want to keep it for the rest of his life and tell his kids the story of how he won it. Ladies, the choice is yours.

It Is Your Fault I Let You Down

In 2015, I was very close with my neighbor's son. He was sentenced to 5 years in prison due to a few bad decisions. I remember the day of the sentencing was a sad day for his mother. She witnessed her son stand before the court and plead guilty to all charges. She was at a loss for words. All she could say repeatedly was, "I am so confused" and "I just do not understand". The sentence hit her like a brick in the chest. She broke down crying as the bailiff took her son away. On the ride home, I listened to her tell me all about him dating back to his childhood. Desmond's father passed when he was much younger. Raised by his mother alone, he was such a mother's boy. He was a good kid she said. He always bought home good grades and received accolades for his behavior. He was very active in church, He even sang in the choir. She laughed and then said he was a terrible singer, but he was so passionate and courageous the entire church cheered him on. It was good to see her smile.

When he was 15, he came to her and told her that he wanted to go to college and become a judge. She was taken back this statement. She said, "How many 15-year-olds want to be a judge?" They would go to the local library together every Tuesday and check out books on law enforcement and read up on state judges, and they continued this for a year. She said over that year she watched as his vision to be a judge grew stronger and stronger. She just knew that nothing was going to stop her son from becoming a judge. Later, one of his mother's co-workers invited them both to a fundraising basketball game held by the city police officers. Her co-worker's husband was a retired police officer. He was excited to meet Desmond, and he introduced him to all his fellow officers. Desmond even got the opportunity to meet one of the local judges in the book he read.

Desmond was very excited that he met the judge. He could not wait to tell his mother, but that was placed on hold because his mother was conversing with one of the officers she met through her co-worker. Desmond sat back and watched the game. He did not get the opportunity to talk to his mother about his experience until they were in the car on the ride home. Desmond suppressed how he was feeling because his mother seemed happy. He simply told her he had a really good time. That Tuesday was the first Tuesday that he and his mother did not go to the library. Desmond found out by eavesdropping on his mother's phone call that she met with that officer after work for coffee, and by the time his mother arrived home, the library was closed.

After 3 weeks of not attending the library, Desmond lost interest in going. It was a Friday evening when Desmond was returning home after school. He walked into the house and saw his grandmother and the officer sitting at the kitchen table. He greeted his grandmother and shook the officer's hand. He then walked to his mother's room to find her getting ready for an evening out.

He hugged his mother and told her he was happy for her; she smiled. Desmond then went to his room conflicted with emotions with no knowledge how to channel them. His mother had not dated since the passing of his father, so on one hand, he was happy for his mother, and on the other, he was also very angry. Desmond felt as If he was losing his mother. This feeling only grew stronger as his mother's feelings for the officer increased, and he began to see less and less of his mother.

Desmond realized that his mother no longer came directly home after work, so he decided that it was no point in him continuing to come directly home after school. He started hanging out with the kids after school and enjoyed it. It was not long until Desmond got mixed up with the wrong people, and that decision changed him completely. The day Desmond decided to join his new friends as they burglarized several the homes in the community did not end the way he expected. They entered the home of a retired military man. The teenagers were unaware that the veteran was home that evening. He was working on his bike in the shed behind his home. He saw the teens entering his home on his security monitor in the shed. He quickly called the police and meet the intruders at his front door with his gun. The police arrived shortly after, and all the teens were arrested and taken into custody.

We took the very first chance we got to go visit Desmond. The visit started off nice but took a turn for the worst when his mother asked him to help her understand. Desmond grew angry and refused to answer, so his mother asked again and again, and still Desmond sat quietly. Responding out of pure frustration, his mother began to explain to him how she had a better plan for him, how disappointed she was, and how she thought she knew him. "How she thought she knew him" seemed to trigger a rage of fire within Desmond as he yelled, "You don't know me!" He said that was the problem. She thought she knew him. Desmond then laughed and said, "You disappointed? Well, it's your fault I let you down." His mother with a confused look on her face asked, "My fault?" Desmond said "Yes! You stopped talking to me."

I completely understood what Desmond was attempting to say. This made me think about relationships of all kind. Any two individuals in a relationship unknowingly can have this same issue. We typically meet someone, and the first thing we do is attempt to get to know them. What Desmond was saying to his mother is she wouldn't feel so disappointed if she would stop thinking she knew him and knew what he was capable of doing. She obviously did not know that. The moment you think you know someone you have just opened the door for them to disappoint you. Can you fully get to know someone? The answer is no! You will never get to know someone fully. You may know a lot about a person, but you will never truly know him or her. Life is about choices and decisions. We make choices, and we are forced to live with our decisions. You are the choices you make, and the outcomes of those decisions can change you. Think about the individual you are getting to know. How long has he or she been on this earth? A long time, right? That person could have been on this earth anywhere from 18-50 years, yet tomorrow is a day that he or she has never seen.

Tomorrow presents new challenges, choices, and decisions that we must make. Our decisions shape who we are, which means that all that person's decisions in the past that have made him or her who he or she is today can be altered with one decision made tomorrow. You can know me extremely well today and be completely shocked at who I am tomorrow. As for Desmond and his mother, she figured she knew her son very well. The two of them spent so much time together over the years. However, his mother stopped communicating as much when the officer came into the picture. Desmond felt neglected and began to make different decisions that would alter who he was as a person altogether. To her knowledge, her son was not a burglar, but the decisions he made molded him to be just that.

For example, this book is going to surprise a lot of people that I have known for several years, and I am sure the think they know me, but they do not know me to be an author. Think about that for a second. This book wouldn't come to them as much of a surprise if they had been communicating me. They would have known that I made the choice to write a book, and by that decision, I became an author. The secret is to communicate and try to get to know each other every day. The moment one gets complacent and comfortable thinking that he or she knows someone is the moment that person lets you down, but remember, it's your own fault!

What if I told you that you can control your reality?

Have you ever felt that situations in life, especially dating, love, sex, and marriage can be extremely complicated? The author feels that a large percentage of the complication in life is complicated by us because of our perspectives, behaviors, and decisions.

If only we had alternative views that allowed us to look at the situations from different perspectives, which could alter our behavior and decisions, change the reality of a situation, and result in different outcomes.

In this book, that is what Terry Strickland, Jr. is going to do for you. He will offer you an alternative view that will allow to visit a few chapters in your life that may be complicated, and the views of the author will allow you to view them from a different perspective.

This book is guaranteed to make you say, "Wow! I never thought about it like that."

By reading this book and receiving the alternative views, you will be empowered to offer the people in your life a different perspective that could possibly alter their behaviors and change the reality of all parties involved.

Terry Strickland, Jr. is a dynamic motivational speaker, loving husband, and a dedicated father who delivers a powerful message in hopes of educating women and coaching up men by offering his alternative views to change their perspectives.

Made in the USA
Columbia, SC
05 May 2020